D1331243

7 0000000225061

Out on a Ledge

Enduring the Lodz Ghetto, Auschwitz, and Beyond

Eva Libitzky
Fred Rosenbaum

An Ashley Creek Book
Wicker Park Press, Ltd.

Out on a Ledge

Wicker Park Press, Ltd.
P.O. Box 5318
River Forest, IL 60305
Phone: 773-391-1199
Fax: 312-276-8109
E-mail: editors@wickerpress.com
Website: www.wickerpress.com

Copyeditor: June Brott
Proofreader: Megan Trank
Design: Eric Triantafillou
Cover photos:
    Eva Libitzky: photographer unknown
    Paris Hotel in Prague: Dorothy Shipps
    Lodz Ghetto: USHMM
Author photo of Fred Rosenbaum: Randy Licht

Distributed in Canada by
Scholarly Book Services,
127 Portland Street, 3rd Floor
Toronto, Ontario, Canada M5V 2N4

Distributed in the United Kingdom and Europe by
Roundhouse Publishing Ltd.,
Atlantic Suite, Maritime House
Basin Road North,
Hove, East Sussex BN41 1WR
United Kingdom

Typeset in Chaparral Pro and Apex Serif
Printed in the United States

To my son, Moses,
for preserving the memory of the family I lost,
as a legacy for the family I have.

—E.L.

Table of Contents

Foreword

I NORMALLY BEGIN READING SURVIVORS' memoirs with trepidation. I am about to embark on a journey through a world of darkness and I don't quite know how all-enveloping the darkness and how skilled the guide who will bring me on that journey. I also understand that the story I am to read is not abstract history; it is not about Six Million but about one of those Six Million and the world she inhabited. I am also hesitant because if I am disappointed in the work, it may seem as if I am dismissive of the life that is embodied in that work.

I began reading this volume with confidence because I had read earlier books by Fred Rosenbaum, who has a unique capacity to meld his skill as a writer with the story of the survivor. I knew he would not impose his voice or his agenda on hers.

When Fred approached me to write this foreword, I recalled our meeting the previous summer at the Cracow Jewish Culture Festival and particularly the evening we spent at the joyous concert in Kazimierz Square, the once-vital center of the Jewish community. Surrounded by good food and wonderful music, I met Moses and Ellie, two of Eva's children, and caught a glimpse of their mother's story, including her improbable life after the Holocaust as a chicken farmer in Colchester, Connecticut, a backwater town between Hartford and New London.

Like most memoirs, *Out on a Ledge* has three natural divisions: *before*, *during*, and *after*. First we meet Eva as the charming daughter of pious, prosperous Chasidim in the industrial city of Lodz. Then we witness her imprisonment in the ghetto, the longest-lasting one in Poland, and her deportation to and ordeal in Auschwitz. Finally, we encounter her after the war, trying to learn her family's fate, recover in the DP camp, and adjust to America.

The title of Eva's life story calls to mind the Chasidic Master Reb Nachman of Bratzlav's teaching: "the world is a narrow bridge; and most essentially one must not fear at all." Borrowing from Reb Nachman, Martin Buber held that difficult truths are to be found by walking a "narrow ridge," knowing that one can fall into the abyss on either side. Throughout her life Eva precariously balances herself on a narrow "ledge," separating one world from another. She goes from the world of her childhood, where God's presence was to be found, and loving, protective parents were ever-present, to the world of Lodz and Auschwitz where parents are killed and God is ever more absent. She journeys from Europe in all its darkness to America with all its opportunity. She evolves from an innocent child into a wise adult in response to the extreme suffering that has come her way.

Eva was a dutiful girl in a religious household, but shares with us the qualms she felt in that loving but confining world. In interwar Europe, the divisions between Jews were often *within* the family. Sitting around the same Shabbes table might be children who were choosing different paths for themselves: Zionists and Bundists, secularists and God-fearers. Contact was retained with those who had left the fold; bonds of love overcame political and ideological divisions. Eva never chose to break with her traditional family, even after her faith was shattered. She does not even reproach her father for his refusal to eat non-kosher meat in the ghetto in order to survive. The events that turned her world upside down began not from within but from without.

Eva vividly portrays the Lodz ghetto, where Mordecai Chaim Rumkowski reigned supreme. Unlike his counterpart, Adam Czerniakow, the Chairman of the *Judenrat* (the Jewish Council) in Warsaw, who permitted multiple centers of influence within the ghetto, Rumkowski tightly controlled everything: housing and commerce, health and culture, even religion. He officiated at weddings and even put his picture on ghetto currency. But Rumkowski also had a strategy: "survival through work." He reasoned that if the ghetto could produce quality goods for the *Wehrmacht* and also make his immediate German supervisor, Hans Biebow, filthy rich, the powers that be would have a stake in keeping the inmates alive. In the midst of squalor, disease, starvation, and the stench of raw sewage, Lodz's Jews got up each morning and slaved until nightfall.

Conditions deteriorated further when Jews from Germany, Luxembourg and Czechoslovakia were brought into the ghetto. 5,000 Gypsies were also incarcerated in one section. By 1941, 40,000 workers were employed in factories run by the Judenrat. But there was little of the smuggling that alleviated hunger in Warsaw and the other ghettos. Rumkowski would not permit it.

Yet the ghetto's impressive productivity and profits did not satiate the Nazis' thirst for blood. During the first five months of 1942, 55,000 Jews and all 5,000 Gypsies were deported and murdered in gas vans at Chelmno. Rumkowski was informed of their fate. More than 2,000 patients were deported to Chelmno from the Lodz hospital, including 400 children and 80 pregnant women. Eighteen patients who tried to escape were shot.

In early September 1942, the Nazis ordered that all children and old people in the Lodz ghetto be rounded up for evacuation. A few weeks earlier in Warsaw, Adam Czerniakow had refused a similar ultimatum, stating: "they have asked me to kill the children with my own hands, this I cannot do." He swallowed cyanide rather than sign the deportation order. But Rumkowski acted differently: he demanded that the parents in the ghetto surrender their children.

Such were the conditions under which Eva lived. But she was young, with both an inner life of self-discovery and an outer one of harsh brutality. The two were linked: any moment could be her last. And the response of some young people was to live more intensely, to deepen personal relationships, in order to lessen the horrific impact of what was happening externally.

Listen to her words as her innocence begins to fall away during her first love:

We would hold hands, the first time I'd ever touched a male outside my family. And then we'd sneak out to one of the seldom-used passageways connecting the compound to share caresses and to kiss...Given my sheltered background it was electrifying... He reached my mind, body, and soul.

Life in the shadow of death is still life, made all the more precious by its fragility. The reader will appreciate why, until now, the story of this first love and first marriage was never shared with Eva's family. It remained in the zone of the unspoken, perhaps also the untainted.

Rumkowski's strategy worked for a time, but even he could

not anticipate the degree to which the Germans were pursuing both the War Against the Jews and the World War. With time running out, with the Red Army in Poland, the Lodz Ghetto was liquidated before its liberation. Along with its other inmates, Eva was deported to Auschwitz.

Upon arrival she was separated from her family. Young and able-bodied, she faced "selection." She describes how pain and self-pity led to anger and determination:

> *I was in such physical agony that it was hard to think about any-thing but my empty stomach, parched mouth, or aching bones—and the revenge to be taken later...The first stirrings of my will to live...were born out of a desire to get back at them.*

Women survivors in particular sometimes speak of the surrogate families they formed: camp sisters who banded together and made the near-impossible conditions a bit more bearable. This was essential for Eva during her forced march from Auschwitz. When she fell to the ground, they picked her up. "We won't let you die here," they cried.

She was transported from Auschwitz to a subcamp of Flossenberg and later to Theresienstadt where liberation came only on May 5, 1945. But for Eva, "to rejoice wholeheartedly was impossible; too much had been destroyed."

The reader will be grateful for her many insights into the way back from destruction. She reentered the world by helping others as a nurse, but she also had to confront the magnitude of her own loss. Ultimately she found a new life in the company of other survivors with whom she shared so much that words were not needed.

Eva stresses the need for friendship and companionship, and even the desperation that led some survivors to marry virtually anyone, for they could not bear to be alone. Like marriage, other imperatives were childbirth, "my way of defying Hitler" Eva writes, and immigration, for staying in Germany was out of the question.

"From rags to riches" is a favorite American motif, yet Eva's story does not fit into this mythic mold. Married in the DP camp, she came to America with her husband, Martin, himself a survivor of the Lodz Ghetto and Auschwitz, and they struggled for decades.

In remote Colchester, Connecticut they barely made a living. Life on the land meant rising early in the morning, working seven days a week, cleaning up barns and chicken coops, the cold of winter, the heat of summer. There is little romance in her depiction of these years and one almost senses the self-reliance and fierce individuality of the Yankee farmer. Martin works two jobs and is frequently away; the responsibility for raising children is mostly Eva's. One easily detects her isolation and loneliness.

Much later, life gets easier when they move twenty-five miles from Colchester to Manchester, from a hardscrabble rural existence to middle class suburban respectability. Due to the uncanny quirks of Jewish geography, I have personally known both of those communities and some of the survivors who touched the Libitzkys' lives. As a young professor at Wesleyan University, my family lived on a lake near Colchester in an even smaller country town, and my former wife's family lived in Manchester for generations. So I appreciate the stories they must have shared with each other, and their pride in their children, grandchildren, and great-children. Such was their triumph. Such was the life of survivors in post-war America.

There is a current chapter in Eva's story. In retirement, she and Martin moved to South Florida, now the home of the second largest community of survivors in the United States. She has mastered her past by becoming a witness, a teacher, in classrooms of American students who see in her a symbol of strength and resilience. They learn from her one of life's most important lessons: not every defeat must be final; one can overcome, and that which one cannot overcome, one must have the courage to endure. It is a lesson that will serve these youngsters well as they face the vicissitudes of their lives without quite appreciating the many gifts that they have received.

Alzheimer's has taken Martin's memory, which may have given Eva a sense of urgency to search her own. The journey was long and painful, but its telling is honest and piercing, unsentimental and yet deeply moving.

Michael Berenbaum
Los Angeles, California

Prologue
Prague, June 1945

IT SOUNDED LIKE HALF A platoon of drunken Soviet soldiers was bounding up the stairs, heading for our room. Their heavy footsteps broke the midnight quiet. "Girls! Girls!" they shouted excitedly in Russian. We bolted the door but they began banging on it with their fists. How long before it would give way?

I was sharing that fourth-floor hotel room with three other Jewish women from Lodz, like me all in their early twenties. It was like living in a fairyland after what we'd just been through— five and a half years in the Lodz ghetto, Auschwitz-Birkenau, a slave labor camp, and finally Theresienstadt, where I weighed only sixty-five pounds. There we had heard that many Lodzers were in nearby Prague. So after our liberation we journeyed to the capital in search of our loved ones. The Czechs were generous to survivors, providing us food, clothing, and even housing in the famous Paris Hotel. The excruciating pain of daily existence gave way to a springtime of pleasure and elegance. But were we now about to suffer yet another horror, at the hands of another occupying army?

I looked out the large casement window at street below, a drop of seventy or eighty feet. Then, directly below, I noticed a metal-covered ledge, only a few inches wide that seemed to run the length of the hotel's exterior. Five Jewish guys from Lodz, whom we had met only two days earlier, roomed together a few doors down the corridor from us. It was a terrifying prospect, but if we could balance ourselves on the ledge, holding on to the stone gargoyles for support, we'd be able to make our way to the window of our five male friends—and to safety. Carefully, I stepped onto that narrowest of pathways and the others followed. We moved slowly, our backs to the cityscape below, our hands against the rough stone walls.

I had faced mortal danger many times before; I would encounter different kinds of adversity in the years ahead. But with determination and resourcefulness, loyal friends and a lot of luck, I've prevailed.

Time and again, I've had to take the initiative in order to survive. This may seem surprising because until my late teens I was nurtured by pious parents and grandparents in a Chasidic sect, a way of life that many associate with passivity, especially on the part of females. But in fact, my upbringing turned out to be a source of strength.

1 Tateh's Little Girl

MY PARENTS HAD TRIED FOR ten years to have a child before my brother was born in 1918. I came along six years later in 1924. Among traditional Jews a decade of barrenness was considered grounds for divorce. Some believed it was a curse from God and a few prominent rabbis held that such misfortune required the dissolution of a marriage even if the couple still wanted to remain together.

I can hardly imagine the anxiety my mother and father must have felt as that ten-year mark neared, or the joy they shared when mother gave birth to Moishe. My parents ran a successful business and were respected by Jew and non-Jew alike, but without any offspring their lives would have been ruined. Even after I entered the world, our family of only two kids was considered very small; in our circles a brood of seven or eight was typical. But with a boy and a girl my father had finally fulfilled the Biblical obligation to be fruitful and multiply. So Moishe and I were adored by our parents.

For generations both sides of my family were devout members of the largest Chasidic sect in Poland, the Gerer, based near Warsaw in the town of Ger, with tens of thousands of followers throughout the country. We lived in Lodz but were intensely loyal to the *rebbe*, Abraham Mordecai Alter, who sat in splendor in his *hoyf,* or court, a complex of buildings on the banks of the Vistula, seventy miles away.

The rebbe was our unquestioned guide as we sought favor in the eyes of the Lord. With zeal, we prayed, studied, and tried to perform acts of loving-kindness. Needless to say, we also strictly observed the Sabbath and holidays, meticulously keeping the kosher laws. Every detail of life was regulated—the clothes we wore, the words we spoke, and even how we walked down the street.

My own faith ran deep. I believed in the stories of the Bible and the magical powers of the rebbe. I had no doubt the God of Israel rewarded and punished us depending on our actions. Even so, I sometimes felt my life was overly disciplined and controlled—that we exceeded God's requirements. On Shabbes I wasn't allowed to comb my hair because if I accidentally pulled out a strand it would be considered work. How could this be considered a sin, I wondered, even as a little girl.

More often, though, I delighted in heavenly moments that only such a religious childhood could bring. On Friday night, when my father and brother came back from the *shtiebl,* or prayer house, for the Sabbath meal, it was as if the angels entered with them. Moishe wore the silk hat reserved for serious Talmudists and father had on the *shtreimel,* or round fur head-cover, made of mink. They both wore *kapotehs,* long black frock coats with a sash around the waist to symbolize the distinction between the higher and the lower, the sacred and the profane. A spirit of holiness descended upon the house as father, *Tateh*, as I called him in Yiddish, blessed my brother and me and chanted a tribute to my mother. With an *oyrech*, a needy guest he always brought home, we'd eat heartily of chicken soup and noodles, stuffed carp, and *tzimmes*, or honey-baked carrots. My mother baked challah and cake as well. Afterwards, we'd sing the Chasidic melodies for hours. The next evening, Mameh didn't want to let go of Shabbes; I can still see her now, sitting by the window and softly singing Yiddish tunes.

Every season had its special treat. In the fall, I loved eating outdoors in our *sukkah*, an arbor covered with pine branches, and I'd decorate it with chains of multi-colored paper. We invited our Jewish neighbors to join us. During Chanukah, we lit our three-foot-high silver menorah with special olive oil from the Holy Land. In the midst of that holiday we looked ahead to Passover. In clay pots we preserved *schmaltz*, or goose fat, and beets for borscht, which we'd enjoy four months later. Tateh and Moishe baked their own strictly kosher matzahs, which were hard and thick, unlike the matzahs you get today in America. For the holiday of Shavuos, in late spring, my mother filled the house with palm fronds and fragrant lilacs and served sweet, creamy blintzes and rich cheesecake.

Although most Chasidic girls didn't receive a great deal of Jewish learning, Tateh treated me almost like a boy. After I turned three, he hired a *melamed*, or schoolteacher, to come to our home and tutor me and thus I received training in Bible and prayers even before I started attending a Jewish school five afternoons a week. Although it wasn't required for a female of any age, I *davened*, or prayed, three times a day, said the *Sh'ma* before going to sleep, and if I missed my prayers for any reason, my conscience bothered me. I even spoke a little Hebrew with my big brother. We weren't supposed to use the holy tongue in everyday conversation but we did anyway, teasing one another in the language of the Bible.

Yet nothing came close to the pleasure I felt on Shabbes, sitting in Tateh's lap and watching him beam with pride as I recited portions of the *Chumash*, the five books of Moses, or translated them from Hebrew into Yiddish. I felt smart, and pretty, and most of all a good daughter; there was nothing I wouldn't do for him. He had many pet names for me—I was his kitten, his lamb, his Chavele, or little Chava—but one of them really said a lot: *Zaddaikesta*, a little female holy person, a modified version of how the rebbe, or *Zaddik*, himself might be called.

And the rebbe was on father's mind all the time. As much as the Jewish festivals meant to our family life, Tateh, often with Moishe, would sometimes leave my mother and me at home during Rosh Hashana, Yom Kippur, and other holidays to make a pilgrimage to the Gerer rebbe. Females were not welcome there, but I found out from my brother what this journey involved. The men would travel by train first to Warsaw and then transfer to a special rail line, constructed at the turn of the century with funds

The Gerer Rebbe, Abraham Mordecai Alter, walking in a Polish resort town with his followers trailing behind him. (courtesy USHMM)

provided by the rebbe at that time, Yehuda Aryeh Alter. His son, Abraham Mordecai, would take over in 1905 beginning a tenure of more than four decades. In fact, the rebbe's family dynasty reached back to the mid-1800s when the sect was founded by Abraham Mordecai's legendary great-grandfather.

There were thirty Chasidic sects in Lodz alone, each devoted to its own charismatic leader, distinguished by his wondrous deeds. And while the Gerer despised other forms of Judaism—you can imagine what they thought of the Reform movement—their deepest contempt was reserved for the rebbes of rival Chasidic groups, most notably the Aleksander (based in Aleksandrow, near Lodz), who followed a Zaddik, or righteous man, named Isaac Menachem Danziger. The Gerer were more scholarly and the Aleksander more mystical, but the two groups were so similar in dress and behavior, in prayers and beliefs, that few outsiders could tell them apart. Yet to us Gerer there was a world of difference: the Aleksander rebbe was a fraud and an ignoramus and neither he nor his deluded followers could be trusted. It was best to shun them.

Our rebbe, by contrast, was a prophet and a miracle worker, and to be in his presence was to be close to the divine. So on Jewish festivals many thousands of Chasidim, like my father and brother, would overwhelm the tiny town of Ger, lodging with locals or in boarding houses and sleeping as many as ten to a room. There was usually such an overflow crowd in the rebbe's synagogue that some fervent youths had to attend the service while tied by their waists to a rope suspended from the tall iron posts that held up the ceiling. Afterwards, there would be a lot of singing and dancing—and drinking; away from their womenfolk and home towns, the Chasidic pilgrims often let loose.

Others came to Ger for an audience with the rebbe. He was beseeched for a favor, a blessing, or advice on everything from medical problems to marriage proposals. He might be asked to settle a quarrel or analyze a business deal. Men submitted petitions to the *gabbai*, the rebbe's chief of staff, on a *kvittel*, a piece of notepaper, and it could take days until the wonder man agreed to a meeting. Even some Christians thought him godly and sought his counsel.

The rebbe was mobbed by his disciples everywhere he went, and to sit at his *tisch*, or table, and share a meal with him was an honor reserved only for a select few, who surely paid a lot for the privilege. But anyone willing to risk being trampled in a mad rush could try for the holy *shrayim*, the Zaddik's leftover food. One of my cousins was long admired for once diving under the table to retrieve a morsel that had fallen from the rebbe's plate.

The rebbe visited Lodz only once that I know of, for the funeral of one of his relatives, and another mob scene ensued with boys climbing trees in order to get a view of him. But even when he remained in his court in Ger, he ruled our lives. This became all too clear to me one Thursday night when, at the age of nine, I became violently ill with fever, abdominal pain, and vomiting. The next day my frightened father summoned two prominent surgeons to examine me. They told him my appendix had ruptured. My life was in peril, they said, and they recommended an immediate operation at the best children's hospital in Lodz—a Catholic institution. To further complicate matters, it was now close to sunset and Shabbes was about to begin.

My parents were frantic—only half a year earlier one of their nieces had died of appendicitis. Father was prepared to take me to the hospital by droshky, a four-wheeled horse-drawn carriage, a desecration of the Sabbath but justified in this case because it was a matter of life and death. Yet he didn't feel he could go forward with something as serious as an operation—on any day of the week—without the rebbe's blessing. His brother-in-law felt the same way. When my cousin Bronka urgently needed her tonsils removed, Uncle Yankel delayed the medical procedure until approval came from Ger.

So Tateh called the rebbe—on Friday evening. Because we had no phone (few homes in Poland did before the war), he went around the corner to a tobacco shop where for twenty zlotys, the sum it would take to feed a large family for a week, he placed the long distance call.

Not surprisingly, the rebbe was unavailable. All Tateh could do was reach a "Shabbes goy," a non-Jewish assistant, who was allowed to answer the phone. Father explained the dire situation and was promised that the rebbe would receive the message. With the further assurance that the tobacconist would be in earshot of the phone all night if necessary, and summon him when the return call came through, Tateh walked back home. He waited and he prayed.

Hours went by. Tormented by the sharp pain, delirious from the raging fever, I screamed my head off while my parents and brother brought me liquids and cold compresses.

I've long wondered what father was thinking as he watched my life slipping away but I've never blamed him for the way he handled the crisis. Yes, the aura surrounding the Chasidic rebbes often blinded their followers, but Tateh had lived with that from the day he was born. How could I expect him not to have sought the Zaddik's blessing in the midst of such an emergency? Tateh was a genuine man of faith and perhaps thought of the rebbe's namesake, the patriarch Abraham, whom God spared at the last instant from sacrificing his beloved Isaac.

Not until the middle of the night did word come from the rebbe that it was God's will to follow the doctors' orders. At dawn I was driven in a droshky to the Anna Maria Hospital, my agitated parents alongside me. Antibiotics were not yet in use in this era so my chances of survival were slim. But a tube was inserted in my abdomen to drain the infected pus and fluid. There was not even intravenous therapy in Poland then, but my mother, an aunt, and a cousin came to the hospital day and night and put drops of water into my mouth hourly. Tateh visited frequently too and gave me permission to eat the non-kosher food like Kielbassa and even bread during Passover. It took three months but I finally got better, came home, and returned to school.

We all regarded my recovery as miraculous and I'm sure father felt that my life was saved because we'd waited through the night for the rebbe's blessing. To Tateh, the Zaddik cured me as much as had the doctor.

Today such thinking may seem like something out of the Middle Ages but my father was not as backward as it sounds. Unlike many Chasidic men, spending nearly all their waking hours in the *Bais Midrash*, the study hall, while their wives worked hard to support a large family, Tateh functioned well in the modern world as a big-city businessman.

We did not live in some isolated shtetl in the countryside, but in Lodz, with almost three-quarters of a million souls, the country's second largest metropolis and its main manufacturing hub. We strolled on broad boulevards, rode the clanking streetcars, and enjoyed electricity and running water, conveniences not commonplace in the small towns. Few Chasidim worked in the noisy textile factories, or debated politics in the coffeehouses, but we felt the pulse of urban life. No Lodzer could remain deaf to the roar of industry or the discontent of the working class.

During my childhood, Jews accounted for almost a third of the inhabitants of Lodz. Nearly a quarter-million strong, we were a distant second to Warsaw but exceeded the Jewish population of Holland, Belgium, and Luxembourg combined. And Lodz

Jewry was a mixed lot. The magnificent synagogue of the Reform Jews, whose wealthy members arrived in fancy carriages, was well known to us and we were aware of Orthodox, Zionists, and Jewish socialists of all stripes.

Beyond that, my family had a lot of interaction with non-Jews because Lodz was a multi-cultural city. It had been part of the Czarist Empire before World War I, so a lot of Russians were there during my parents' youths. The booming textile mills, which increased the town's population about a hundred-fold in the nineteenth century, attracted immigrants from all over Central Europe.

Our district, the pleasant Gorny Rynek section in the southeastern part of town, was by no means a Jewish neighborhood; it was populated mostly by Poles, and ethnic Germans known as *Volksdeutsche*. Along with some Jews, they were the patrons of my father's large, thriving grocery market at 9 Napiorkowskiego and he was on good terms with his customers. It didn't compare in size to an American supermarket but it seemed enormous to me as a child and for that time and place our store was huge; after the war it would be carved into three separate retail businesses. I loved helping out, opening the big burlap sacks and sorting the items either for display, or storage in a cavernous space just beneath the ceiling. When we were short-handed during the busy times before the holidays, we recruited some of my cousins, too.

At least once a week, Tateh would go across town to a vast wholesale market, the Alte Marek, and purchase goods in bulk to be delivered later by horse-drawn wagons. We carried staples such as flour and sugar, rice and beans, and potatoes and kasha but we also offered endless varieties of Asian tea, South American coffee, and Mediterranean chicory. There were luxuries like canned sardines and fancy tobaccos. Even during the Depression business was brisk.

My mother worked alongside Tateh in the store. Unlike many traditional Jews of their generation, who were comfortable only in Yiddish, they both spoke Polish and German fluently. Exceptionally good was my mother's Polish. Although her name was Chana, she was dubbed Anja by her Catholic customers, and her relatives called her that as well. My folks expressed their gratitude to their non-Jewish patrons at Christmas time by handing out gifts: chocolate Santa Clauses that came in different sizes—the better the customer, the larger the Santa Claus his family received.

The image of my father running that store is before my eyes even today. He wore the *peyes,* the traditional ear-locks of the Chasidim, but very short and tucked behind his ears while he conducted business dressed in a suit. His beard was not long either. My mother wore the *sheitel*, of course, the wig that a married ultra-Orthodox or Chasidic woman puts on to discourage

My uncle Yankel Katz. Few Chasidic Jews posed for pictures, but Yankel frequently traveled abroad for business and needed this passport photo. My father dressed similarly. (courtesy Bernice Sobotka)

Our home and business on Napiorkowskiego as it looks today. (The street has been renamed Przybyszewski.) Our grocery store occupied the entire ground floor. We had one apartment behind the store on the left and another directly above the two stores on the right.

advances from men other than her husband. But it was stylish and she donned a nice, long-sleeved, multi-colored dress—it came below her stocking-covered knees but not to her ankles—and an apron over that. Father always had a large volume of the Talmud close at hand and would delve into it if he had a few minutes between customers. Other religious men stopped by to put some coins in one of the many *pushkas*, or tin charity boxes, which filled an entire wall of shelves. Then the men would stay and talk but the topic of conversation was politics as much as it was Torah.

If the store was where we met the outside world, our home was where Judaism alone reigned. We occupied two apartments in the same big building as our business. One apartment was on the ground level directly behind the store. It was fairly plain and we took our meals there during the week. A staircase, which my parents installed, led to a separate upstairs apartment, which was quite elegant and included a spacious kitchen where my mother prepared our bountiful Sabbath and holiday meals. We always had a maid and when it was a non-Jewish girl, a *shikseh,* Mameh wouldn't let her do much more than wash dishes, or peel potatoes lest she unknowingly violate *kashrus,* the complex set of kosher laws. The large living-dining room, lit by a crystal chandelier, had upholstered chairs set around an oval mahogany table. Near it, a waist-high wrought-iron stand held a lovely porcelain bowl and pitcher for the ritual of washing one's hands before eating. Just inside the doorway, behind glass doors, was my father's *Gemurah shrank,* a deep closet of shelves for his many handsomely bound religious books. Each apartment had only a single bedroom, though, and my brother and I shared the one upstairs until I was around eleven. Then he moved into my parents' bedroom downstairs and my mother moved up to mine.

In the summers I left home, leaving behind the heat and soot of the industrial city, for the sweet-smelling air and colorful wildflowers of the countryside. The horse-and-wagon ride itself, on tree-lined roads alongside birch and pine groves, was soothing. I stayed with my father's parents, Eli and Tovah Gerszt, near their home in Zdunska Wola, about twenty-five miles from Lodz. My grandfather, who was born in the mid-1860s in Lutomiersk, a village even closer to Lodz, must have pursued a business opportunity in Zdunska Wola after he and my grandmother married in her birthplace of Lask, yet another nearby hamlet. By the eve of World War II, Zdunska Wola had about 15,000 people, about half of them Jews, and, typical of this region, it was a stronghold of the Gerer Chasidim. For a couple of months each year, my grandparents rented a farmhouse a few miles out of town, owned by Polish peasants who moved to a shack on their property to accommodate the family of vacationing Jews. *Bubbe,* as grandmother is known in Yiddish, made wonderful meals and took me on walks through the forests and I didn't have a care in the world. *Zayde*, or grandfather, came every Friday afternoon to spend Shabbes with us.

My grandparents Gerszt, each barely five feet tall, were unusual among Chasidic couples in showing a lot of affection for one another in public even in their old age; we called them the lovebirds. They had seven children and around 1908 their second-oldest son, Shlomo, went to Lodz to start a household with his new bride, Chana Katz, my mother. This had to be considered an excellent match because it joined two leading Gerer families, one from the city and the other from a nearby small town. My Zayde Abraham Katz originally owned the grocery store on Napiorkowskiego, and although he was retired when I was growing up, he visited the place often, sitting in a special chair reserved for him; the business had probably gone to my father as part of the dowry.

Around the time my father married, three of his brothers moved to Kalisz, about thirty-five miles northwest of Zdunska Wola and sixty miles west of Lodz, where they operated a highly lucrative business as wholesalers of tailoring supplies. Kalisz, about twice the size of Zdunska Wola, was a thriving textile center, specializing in lace making, and the Gerszt brothers, all devout Gerer Chasidim, made a good living by supplying the town's many factories and retailers and investing the profits in real estate.

While my father's family was from outlying towns, my mother's had been in Lodz for at least two generations. She was one of four children of Abraham and Ruchel Katz, and my tall, distinguished grandfather was not only a prominent business-man and communal leader, but also a Talmud scholar. Chasidic couples sometimes asked his advice on marriage and family problems. I came over to his beautiful home almost every day on my way between my Polish and Jewish schools. Bubbe Katz was a phenomenal baker and cook—she actually attended cooking school at the age of sixty-five—and usually had a big, delicious cookie for me. On holidays the entire Katz clan—including fifteen grandchildren—would gather and share a thick, savory *cholent,* a meat and vegetable stew that had been prepared the day before.

But even at these events it was clear that not everyone in the family was a fervent Chasid. Some of my second cousins showed little interest in Judaism and it seemed they had dropped in just to stuff themselves with Bubbe's fabulous cholent. And Zayde Katz's youngest child, my Tante Bronka, shocked the family by marrying a *ying,* literally a youth but our derogatory term for a non-observant Jew (perhaps shorthand for *grobe* ying, or coarse, ill-mannered youth). The way my family carried on, she might just as well have married a goy. She remained respectful of her parents but it was obvious she'd broken away completely from the Gerer way of life. By coincidence, several of the rebels in the family's younger generation were also named Bronka (including Uncle Yankel's daughter who married a ying in the late 1930s) so a saying was whispered around: "None of the Bronkas are any good."

The Gerer rebbe was worried about the challenges posed to his sect and to Torah-true Judaism in the twentieth century. Unlike his predecessors, he fought back using the tools of the modern world—politics, public relations, and education. Even before the Polish Republic was formed in 1920, our rebbe was one of the founders of Agudas Israel, a powerful organization of Chasidic and ultra-Orthodox Jews (though not including our arch-rivals, the Aleksander Chasidim), which published newspapers and issued manifestos urging Jews to keep the commandments. The rebbe also helped establish Bais Ya'akov, a nationwide network of (mostly afternoon) schools for religious girls, the first time formal Jewish education was offered to females in Eastern Europe.

I attended the one in my neighborhood and studied Hebrew and Yiddish, Bible and prayer, and even some Talmud.

But the major breakthrough was the Aguda's entry into politics. Several of their candidates were elected to the *Sejm*, or Polish parliament, and hundreds served on Jewish community councils throughout the country. Every town had such a governing body, known as a *Gemine* or *Kehilla*, and it controlled key areas of Jewish life including social welfare, kosher slaughtering, Jewish education, religious buildings, and much more. The councils, far more powerful than the Jewish federations in America today, were authorized by the national government in Warsaw to collect taxes from Jews and allocate the funds.

Council members were elected by the Jewish public (although only men could vote) and competition among the dozens of political parties was fierce. The Aguda of course clashed with the anti-religious groups; a bitter enemy was the Bund, which trumpeted socialism and atheism.

In the spring of 1931, the Aguda, propelled by the Gerer Chasidim, won a landslide victory in the Jewish councils of Lodz, Warsaw, Kalisz, Zdunska Wola, and many other cities and towns. How were they able to pull off this coup? Before the balloting, the Aguda demanded that groups like the Bund be banned from voting or holding office, and the Polish government, which feared and hated Jewish leftists in particular, complied. Beyond that, the rebbe's followers stuffed the ballot boxes with the votes of people long dead. The worst irregularities were reported in Lodz. In the end, the Aguda won an absolute majority in our city, fifteen seats out of twenty-nine, results that were officially certified in Warsaw.

My grandfather Abraham Katz was one of those elected on the Aguda slate and our family, paying no attention to the way his party came to power, was thrilled. He and his colleagues now worked hard to strengthen religious institutions while they stripped the funding for leftwing and secular Jewish groups, including YIVO, a prestigious library and research center based in Vilna (and after the war in New York). Such policies further divided and embittered the Jewish community but there was widespread agreement about one thing—the high priority the Aguda gave to fighting poverty; nearly half of the Gemine's budget in the Depression-stricken years of the early 1930s went toward relief.

Nevertheless, the Aguda was unpopular with the voters by the next election in 1936. With anti-Semitism on the rise, the majority of Jews could not forgive the party for its earlier deal with the Polish government to exclude the Bund from the electoral process. With an Aguda defeat all but certain, the regime in Warsaw simply postponed indefinitely the Gemine election rather than see other Jewish parties gain control.

Zayde Katz, now around seventy, no longer served on the council. But he remained active in the Aguda and forged a political alliance with a wily Gemine member of the General Zionist Party, Mordecai Chaim Rumkowski, who had also been elected in 1931. Later, during the Nazi occupation, he would have the power of life and death over all the Jews of Lodz.

In the late 1930s, Rumkowski had to break ranks with his own party in order to cooperate with the dominant Aguda, now widely considered a puppet of the dictatorial government in Warsaw. Nor was it easy for my grandfather and his religious colleagues to find common ground with a Zionist politician.

Most Chasidic and ultra-Orthodox Jews staunchly opposed Jewish nationalism. They believed the return to the Holy Land would come only with the messiah; it was sinful to try to force God's hand. On top of that, they knew that most Zionists did not feel bound by Jewish law. Yet on this point as so many others, the

Gerer rebbe adjusted somewhat to the changing times and supported the growing Jewish community in Palestine. He stunned other Chasidic leaders, and even many of his own followers, by visiting Palestine six times before the war and once remaining for half a year. In 1936, he wanted to make *aliyah*, as immigration to the Holy Land is known, but his devoted flock in Poland, horrified at the prospect of being abandoned by their Zaddik, successfully pleaded with him to return to Ger. In 1940 a huge bribe and a multinational cloak-and-dagger operation would spirit him out of Nazi-occupied Warsaw to Jerusalem. From his new headquarters in Mea Sha'arim, he led the sect until his death eight years later, around the time of Israeli independence. Of course, all of this proved to the Aleksander Chasidim that their rebbe was the true Zaddik because, as they never tired of saying, *he* stayed with his flock and was martyred with his family in Treblinka.

As a sheltered schoolgirl, I was barely aware of such political and philosophical controversies swirling around me; only much later did I piece together the role of the Gerer Chasidim in prewar Poland. But it was clear even to me that modernity was making major inroads into the traditional society of my parents' generation. Although my brother studied all day in a *cheder,* or Jewish elementary school, and later in a yeshiva, I had a fairly well-rounded education, attending a Polish public school in the morning—proudly wearing my uniform, a black dress with white collar and cuffs—and Bais Ya'akov in the afternoon. The quality of both schools was high and I learned Polish, the language of instruction, and math, science, history, geography, and German. I wasn't required to perform any chores around the house, but I put in long hours in the classroom—nine to one at the public school and two to six at Bais Ya'akov.

Although I had a few girlfriends, my closest confidante was my cousin Deborah, a year older than me, and the second youngest of the eight children of my mother's brother, Yankel Katz. Debusha, as we called her, was my soul mate; we shared our fears and hopes about growing up and our longings and frustrations about the world outside the Chasidic cocoon.

We gazed at couples on the street holding hands, we read Polish romance novels, and we grew envious of the way others lived. At the age of fourteen or fifteen, we'd even figured out how babies were made—although we didn't want to believe our own parents could have performed such an act. We had the normal teenage sexual urges and would have liked physical contact with boys. But of course such conduct was strictly taboo and we could only dream about it.

Outside of marriage, the barrier between males and females was insurmountable. When women went to the synagogue, which was seldom for an unmarried female, we sat upstairs in the women's gallery. Separation of the sexes, though, could go far beyond that. My fanatic teenage cousin Hershel wouldn't even sit at his parents' dinner table because of the presence of his sisters; they were girls, after all. In our home, when Tateh's friends dropped by on Shabbes to study a tractate of Talmud, Mameh and I had to leave the room and go into the kitchen even if it was the middle of a meal. My self-sacrificing mother, who accepted father's many holiday pilgrimages to Ger, and who rarely complained about anything, did express resentment about this treatment—exile from her own dining room table. Tateh said he didn't like that custom either but he could not change it in the presence of other men.

What kept me well behaved was the pressure of my father. It was not that I feared harsh punishment from him; far from it, he was gentle and loving. Rather, I was held in check by my own strong feelings of not wanting to disappoint him or my mother, especially through some scandalous act. How could I have any respect for myself, I thought, if I betrayed the trust of such ador-ing parents? Today a misbehaved child might be grounded in his room or have to surrender the car keys. Some kids are spanked or denied supper, but for me, all it took was a disapproving glance from my father and I'd be pained for days.

Yet one time, around age fourteen, I did let him down although it wasn't entirely my fault. Out for a walk on a Sabbath afternoon with Debusha and a couple of other girls, we entered a park and were suddenly approached by a group of boys from our public school. They started talking to us, and we stopped and chatted with them for a few minutes. I knew it was wrong and was shaking with fear but I couldn't bear the embarrassment of walking away by myself. Sure enough, lurking behind the trees were spies whom the Gerer Chasidim had recruited to report wayward children to their parents.

Early that evening, my father said he needed to speak to me in private. I dreaded what would come next. So that we could be alone, he led me out of the upstairs apartment and down to the store, which was still closed before the Saturday night shift. The news about my bad behavior earlier in the day had already reached him, he said gravely. I started denying it but he had all the details, including the clothes I'd worn and the exact spot where the encounter had taken place. I said the boys had initi-ated the contact but he would have none of that. With tears in his eyes he asked if I realized how I'd shamed him. Then I started weeping too, uncontrollably, for nothing in the world could have been worse. I would have preferred his beating the hell out of me, rather than hearing him say I'd disgraced him.

And yet, the temptations of the city were just too great to be passed up, even by a girl like me, so religious and so much in need of parental approval. Debusha and I plotted several misdeeds, just trying to make sure we wouldn't get caught. One conspiracy involved buying an ice cream cone, non-kosher, of course, from a popular store named Rumba, but in the end we had to abort our plan. The creamery, on Piotrkowska Street, Lodz's most fashionable and busiest promenade, was too wide-open a place. Sadly, we concluded that we might be spied upon again. Many years later I found out that Debusha's older sister, one of the backsliding Bronkas, had discretely bought ice cream at Rumba on several occasions.

Debusha and I could not resist the lure of the movies, however, and in 1939 we took the big risk of going to the Polish cinema several times. Merely to be seen in a movie theater would ruin the reputation of a traditional Jewish girl, but we compounded the sin by choosing the Saturday matinee, the only day we were free from school since Bais Ya'akov met on Sundays. Our forbidden forays took a lot of careful planning. Even the cash we saved to buy the tickets would have been suspicious, so I hid the money in a little compartment in the exterior wall of our building behind a metal plate protecting some electrical wiring. We thought the theater near my home was too dangerous so we walked to one in another neighborhood where we were less likely to be recognized. It took just a few seconds at the ticket booth—we knew the times when there'd be no line—and once inside the dark chamber we were safe from prying eyes. Of course the films weren't nearly as explicit as they are today, but we were excited by the tales of adventure and love. I shudder to think of how crushing it would have been had Tateh found out.

Debusha and I had a role model for rebellion, our youngest aunt, Bronka, who had left the fold even before we were born. She was tall and gorgeous, witty and intelligent, and yet even those words don't properly describe her. People were struck most by her magnetic personality; we all said that Bronka could probably get a meeting with the Polish president himself. She dressed nothing like her other older sisters, my mother and my Tante Rivke. Rather, she wore the latest western fashions and walked down the street with flair. Debusha and I were proud when we could be at her side and we noticed how men turned their heads to get a look at her.

Bronka had married a ying, a non-religious Jew, before we were born but we could sense the keen disappointment still felt by her brother and sisters and especially her pious parents. At first, Abraham Katz disowned her. But she was his daughter, after all, and they soon resumed contact. Her non-observant husband was wealthy, having made a fortune in the junk business, but tragically he was also a compulsive gambler. He lost everything at the card tables, even their exquisite home on Piotrkowska Street. Zayde, out of pity, let the penniless Bronka and her daughter stay in his house although he banned her husband except for occasional visits. Meanwhile, my Uncle Yankel, a successful manufacturer's representative, provided his sister money for food and other necessities, and my father helped by co-signing promissory notes for her. But she was not the sort of woman who would be dependent on her family's charity for long. Her husband had died several years before the war, and she went back into the junk business on her own, prospered, and paid off her debts.

I deeply admired my aunt but thought that if I fell in love with a ying, (a remote possibility, of course) I could never bear to cause my parents the kind of distress she had brought upon hers. In any case, it seemed I was destined to marry a Gerer Chasid. After I turned thirteen my father joyfully announced that he'd betrothed me to one of my cousins on his side of the family, a son of Avrum Moishe of Kalisz, the wealthiest of Tateh's four brothers. Their father, my Zayde Gerszt, was dying by then, but Tateh told me grandfather had blessed the *shidduch*, or match, from his deathbed. No doubt the rebbe had given his blessing as well. The engagement would last for three years, my father went on, and we wouldn't tell too many people about it so as not to tempt the evil eye. But he promised to throw a grand wedding party when I'd turn sixteen, in 1940.

Exactly who was my future husband? I had met many cousins on that side of the family during my blissful summers near Zdunska Wola, but contact with the boys was so limited I didn't have a clear image of which one I was supposed to marry. And now that I was engaged, I wouldn't be allowed to see him until I stood under the *chuppah* on my wedding day.

This wasn't an ideal situation but I don't recall being upset by the news. For one thing, I had come to expect an arranged marriage, which brought honor to our family because it meant we could afford a substantial dowry. In fact, one of my cousins had been betrothed while still in the womb. Her father and another Gerer Chasid with a pregnant wife agreed that if one of them should have a girl and the other a boy they'd be joined in matrimony a decade and a half later and that's exactly what happened. In my case, too, my father and uncle had sealed the deal with a handshake and there was no way to back out of it, not that I would ever consider going against my family's wishes. In any event, the marriage was not to take place for three years and I didn't have to think about it for the time being. To my thirteen-year-old mind, three years seemed like an eternity.

2 The Onslaught

MY LIFE HAPPILY REVOLVED AROUND family and school but I was painfully aware of the hatred that most Poles and *Volksdeutsche* harbored for us Jews despite the friendly greetings I often heard from non-Jewish shoppers in our store. Many Jews who lived through inter-war Poland have spoken of a turn for the worse in the mid-1930s, after the death of President Pilsudski, who had protected us; and also the rise of Nazi Germany, which emboldened fascists in Poland. But if there was an earlier period of relative good will, I was too young to detect it. Throughout my entire childhood, I felt insecure in my hometown and uncomfortable as a citizen of my country.

We were a persecuted minority, humiliated not only by thugs, but also by the government and the church at every turn. For example, because we observed Shabbes our store had to remain shut for two days of the week, although we often conducted business for a few hours on Saturday night and through the backdoor on Sunday. I was sometimes the lookout, a crucial job because the police would impose a heavy fine and even a jail sentence if they caught you selling on the Christian Sabbath. On top of that, special taxes were imposed on small businesses, and the tax collectors tended to be especially harsh on the many Jewish merchants in the country. By the late 1930s the government even started phasing out kosher slaughtering; it was declared inhumane after a long series of parliamentary hearings, filled with anti-Semitic insults.

Worst of all, the authorities looked the other way when hooligans beat up Jews in the streets. Because of our distinctive garb, we Chasidim were particularly vulnerable. We ventured out at night only when it was absolutely necessary and even females could be targets; we'd cover ourselves with shawls so as not to attract attention. The most dangerous seasons were Christmas and Easter, but every period was perilous. One of my cousins married into a family that paid the ultimate price. Her husband was severely beaten and her father-in-law killed after they were attacked one evening by Polish brutes. We were horrified but not completely surprised. Fear always hung in the air.

My family was especially worried about my elderly grandparents Katz who lived only a few blocks from us in a large, tastefully furnished apartment with modern conveniences like a flush toilet, which even we didn't have. They were the only Jews in the building and generally tolerated by their neighbors, but rowdy Polish teenagers from a nearby school often gathered in the building's courtyard to taunt *Zayde* and even push him around when he went out. By 1937, the situation got so bad that his children arranged to move him and grandmother out of there, but the only comparable place they could find was far from us. My grandparents' lives were disrupted and my own daily pattern was, too—I could no longer drop by on my way to Bais Ya'akov and visit them as I had since I'd started school. It all seemed terribly unfair but there was nothing we could do about it.

I encountered bigotry myself from Polish schoolgirls with whom I played ball or hopscotch in our courtyard. I thought of them as friends until, without warning, they or their parents would call me a dirty Jew or tell me to go to Palestine.

Much of the prejudice came from the Catholic Church. We were accused of killing Jesus, of course, but also of many other things. The country's leading Cardinal even blamed us for the serious problem of Poland's alcoholism because, he publicly claimed, Jews owned and operated so many taverns. We learned from Uncle Yankel's family about a young Catholic woman who had come from a nearby hamlet to work for them as a maid and was so scared of Jews that she avoided eye contact with her employers. At night, terrified of being raped or killed, she barricaded herself inside her little room by moving the chest of drawers against the door. It was all because the village priest had told her Jews were devils.

In such an atmosphere it was hard to feel patriotic, even though Poland was being threatened by Nazi Germany from one side and the Soviet Union from the other. In late 1938, amidst rising international tensions my brother faced the draft. His only thought was to avoid it at all cost. Many Jewish youths felt the same way but for religious boys like Moishe, military service was especially awful, almost a death sentence. Obviously, there would be no way he could get kosher food or observe the Sabbath. His beard and *peyes* would be cut and still he'd have to endure constant abuse from the other soldiers. He couldn't have survived one day in uniform.

Like so many at that time he tried for a deferment on medical grounds. There was nothing wrong with him so a self-inflicted injury or illness would be the only way to prove himself unfit.

Some young men amputated their trigger fingers, others gave themselves hernias, and no doubt Moishe would have resorted to something like that if necessary. But after discussing all the grim options with my parents, he decided to get sick by eating next to nothing, taking strong laxatives, and staying up all night—for weeks on end. It worked. Even before he got on the scale during the physical exam he was told to go home immediately. Moishe looked so frail the army doctor probably was afraid he'd drop dead right in front of him.

Yet my brother quickly recovered and had even more good fortune by becoming engaged to a girl from our sect. I'd never seen him happier than when the date of his wedding was set— late September 1939.

But before his marriage, the world would be turned upside down. We had no radio but subscribed to a Yiddish newspaper for religious Jews and read of Hitler's annexation of Austria and part of Czechoslovakia. By 1939 the Fuehrer was menacing Poland, demanding the return of lands Germany had lost in the Versailles peace treaty. I didn't follow these developments closely but I remember that talk of war was on everyone's lips.

Well before that, the Gerer rebbe had sounded an alarm. Most rabbis were deaf to the threat of Nazism and counseled the Jews to leave their fate in the hands of God. Our spiritual leader was different, however, and a few years before the war he solemnly prophesied a calamity: "My children, a bitter time is coming." His own extended stay in Palestine seemed to add credibility to his warning.

Uncle Yankel's family of ten actually considered moving to the Holy Land as early as 1937. Like the rebbe, he opposed Jewish statehood yet hoped Jerusalem could provide a refuge from the worsening situation in Europe. Yankel proposed to immigrate by himself and send for his large family later, a plan his

wife, my devout Aunt Reileh, could not accept. Although she was
a dedicated homemaker and a volunteer for charitable causes her
whole life, she had none of the job skills necessary to support her
eight children in Yankel's absence. So that family, like nearly all
my other relatives and friends, stayed in Lodz.

With the Nazi-Soviet pact signed on August 22, 1939,
hostilities seemed almost certain. At the end of the month the
government closed the schools, mobilized the army, and forti-
fied the capital. In Lodz thousands of volunteers, including some
Chasidim, dug anti-aircraft trenches in the summer heat. We all
braced ourselves for the German invasion, which came on September 1.

But what did I know of the meaning of war? To me, a naïve
fifteen-year-old, war was the clash of armies on a far-off battlefield such as I'd seen in romantic movies. It was not the destruction of the civilian population. Of course I was worried to learn
my country had been invaded—I saw enemy planes overhead
and heard explosions in the distance—but I was not in a panic.
After all, my large extended family was all around me, and a store
full of provisions was at our disposal.

During those first days of September, as Wehrmacht armor
roared toward Lodz, less than a hundred miles from the German
border, thousands of Jews fled eastward to Warsaw, Bialystock,
or, even further, to the Soviet Union. Because Nazi planes had
wrecked the railway system, the pitiful refugees went by horse-
drawn carts piled high with whatever belongings they could sal-
vage. Others left Lodz on foot, their bundles on their backs. With
bombs falling all around them, with limited supplies of food and
money, and certainly no support from the Polish population, it
seemed to us that the fugitives had made a very wrong choice.

My family wondered whether the situation was really so
desperate. We had read reports in the Yiddish press and heard

rumors about atrocities against Jews but we thought the stories were probably exaggerated. Despite the Polish anti-Semitism we knew so well, it was hard to grasp that in Germany, a civilized nation, synagogues had been burned and Jewish men sent to concentration camps. We weren't able, or willing, to believe that people were capable of doing such things.

A couple of days before the troops in steel helmets and shiny jackboots marched into Lodz, my grandfather sat with my father in our downstairs apartment behind the store. I overheard their conversation. "It's a *blitzkrieg*," said Abraham Katz, the wisest person I knew, and, for once ignoring the rebbe's words, he insisted, "It will be over in a month and then things will be back to normal. Don't worry." My father nodded and they both agreed that Moishe's marriage would go ahead as planned. Even a Nazi invasion could not postpone a Chasidic wedding.

Our store was looted on the second day of the Nazi occupation. German soldiers stood by as Poles and *Volksdeutsche* burst through the door and grabbed whatever they wanted. Only weeks earlier, some had been good customers, exchanging smiles with my parents. Now they shouted anti-Semitic slurs as they hauled off their plunder. Within a few days every shelf was picked clean. We had enough to eat because earlier we'd stocked our apartments with food, but our business came to a sudden halt.

Next, some neighbors pointed out our house to a few young SS men prowling the streets. They waited for my father and, like predatory animals, pounced on him as soon as he walked out the door. They hit him, kicked him, and tried to pull off clumps of his beard, almost tearing his face in the process. Down on his knees, in the gutter, he was made to perform a series of humiliating calisthenics while Polish bystanders jeered and laughed. Then he was marched off to dig ditches somewhere across town. When he

Near Lodz, invading German troops force a Jewish man to cut the beard of another while Poles look on with satisfaction. (courtesy USHMM)

came home that night aching, bruised, and trembling, we finally had a glimpse into Hitler's new order.

My mother, meanwhile, also worried about my safety. She had just heard of a young girl raped by a gang of Poles in the courtyard of our building. There was nothing any of us could do now except stay home, behind double-bolted locked doors, and hope that the chaos outside would somehow pass.

We were more fortunate than those who had to go out frequently for food and fuel. The emergency distribution centers had long lines of resentful Poles and it took only one of them to spot a Jew and summon German troops to kick that person out of the queue. You could wait many hours just for a loaf of bread and some sugar, my older cousin Bronka told me, and even then go home empty-handed and maybe with a bloodied head as well. With her fair hair and complexion she usually went undetected, but a Jewish man with a beard, or even a woman with Semitic features took a big risk being on the streets. When it was absolutely necessary to venture out, we tried to walk in the shadows.

As bad as the Poles were, we feared even more the many ethnic Germans who lived among us. The Volksdeutsche were about a tenth of the city's population before the war, and a much higher proportion in our neighborhood. Openly hailing the invaders, they gave the Nazi salute, shouted *Heil Hitler*, and displayed the swastika on enormous banners and flags throughout Lodz. They received special privileges and felt they had to prove their loyalty to the Third Reich by tormenting Jews.

And yet we went ahead with my brother Moishe's wedding in late September, a few weeks after our city had fallen and while the war still raged in other parts of Poland. Of course we took many precautions. The ceremony and party were held in the ground-floor home of the bride's uncle, and once everyone was inside we locked the front door. I was designated the lookout and stationed on the sidewalk. If I saw trouble approaching— German soldiers, unruly Poles, or zealous Volksdeutsche—I'd go back into the house, through the window, and tell the dozen or so guests to quiet down. Still, we were able to sing and dance to the music of a fiddler. For a single afternoon we put the war out of our minds and celebrated a *simcha*, a joyous event, the last time I would experience anything like that with my family.

As was the custom among highly traditional Jews, Moishe received *kest*, meaning that he moved into the home of his wife's family, which supported the couple while he continued to study the holy books. I remained with my parents, and my grandfather Katz lived with us, too, while my grandmother stayed with Aunt Rivke and her family. After the war broke out, it wasn't safe for the old folks to be left on their own.

While we cowered indoors that fall of 1939, our basic rights were stripped away one by one. First, the Germans closed all the synagogues in Lodz. Then they froze the bank accounts of Jews, took over all Jewish-owned factories, and banned us from selling textiles or leather. They prohibited Jews from using public transportation or from owning droshkys, pushcarts, or wagons. We weren't allowed to go to parks or movies or even walk on the grand Piotrkowska Street. And we were all required to wear yellow Stars of David, front and back. Those markings helped the authorities enforce the curfew—any Jew caught on the streets between 5 pm and 8 am was arrested.

But as my father's case showed, you could break no rules and still be the victim of violence. In October we heard of Jews being dragged out of the famous Café Astoria and shot on the spot. Others were arbitrarily seized on the streets for forced labor, caught or *chappt*, as we said in Yiddish, never to return.

Perhaps most shocking was the burning of Lodz's two most beautiful synagogues in mid-November, 1939 around the one-year anniversary of *Kristallnacht*, the Night of Broken Glass in Germany, where almost all the synagogues in the country were destroyed. First the Reform Temple on Kosciuszko Boulevard was set ablaze. Its proud dome and stained glass windows, its Torahs and ceremonial objects, were consumed by flames while firemen did nothing but protect the adjacent buildings. On the next night, the stately old Orthodox synagogue on Wolborska Street suffered the same fate.

The *Gemine*, or Jewish community council, so powerful before the war, had fallen into disarray. Many of its members had fled Lodz, including its president, Leib Mincberg of the Aguda party, whom my grandfather Katz knew well because of his own Gemine service earlier in the decade. Into the breach, as early as mid-October, stepped another of Zayde's former colleagues, Chaim Rumkowski.

With the title "Eldest of the Jews," he was appointed by the German occupiers to chair a thirty-man *Judenrat*, or Jewish council, similar to those the occupiers would set up to implement their decrees in almost every Polish city or town they conquered. But Lodz would turn out differently: All the council members except Rumkowski were soon purged, deported, or shot. He alone would wield absolute power over our community for almost five years. Of course even Rumkowski was accountable to the Germans (he had to wear the yellow stars and was beaten by the Gestapo) but we Jews were all accountable to Rumkowski. He would soon establish a Jewish police force, spy web, court system, and prison network all to impose his iron will. "Dictatorship is not a dirty word," he told us in one of his early speeches.

Born and raised in a small town in Russia, Rumkowski had made his mark in Lodz both as a controversial Zionist politician and the head of a large orphanage. There are many versions of how and why the Nazis chose him. One story we Lodzers tell to this day revolves around a misunderstanding of the word *Aelteste,* used by the Germans to mean "eldest" or senior, in the sense of superior in rank, but which a few terrified Jewish officials took to mean "oldest" and thus put forward the sixty-three-year-old Rumkowski.

Mordecai Chaim Rumkowski, Eldest of the Jews. (courtesy USHMM)

Regardless of whether there was any linguistic confusion, more important, I think, was his willingness to take a job few others wanted. Rumkowski was an ambitious, often scheming businessman, political figure, and communal worker who had had mixed success in all his endeavors. Now, late in his life, he wanted to show everyone, including himself, that he possessed great leadership qualities. The Eldest had one prominent physical feature—a thick mane of snow-white hair—that made him appear wise, fatherly and distinguished. In truth, he was uneducated, vengeful, and vain. With the Jews of Lodz obviously facing

Poland after the Nazi conquest, fall 1939.

the worst crisis in their history, he was the one—the *only* one—
he was convinced, who could steer the ship through the storm.

But cocksure though he was, the Germans would take him by
surprise again and again. No doubt Rumkowski was astonished
in November, as were we all, when Lodz and its environs were
annexed to the Reich. Most of the rest of Nazi-occupied Poland
would be a protectorate, treated with the utmost brutality but
at least a "home for Poles" ruled by a military force of thousands
who could not always dominate a population of many millions.
But because Lodz became part of Germany proper, we were in
the grip not only of the SS, but also the Gestapo and the *Kripo*,
the internal criminal police.

Overnight, Polish was banned from the schools and theaters
and the names of all the streets were changed to German. The
residents of upscale Piotrkowska Street found themselves living
on Adolf Hitler Strasse. Our city was renamed Litzmannstadt, in
honor of a German general who had fallen in battle in World War
I. Volksdeutsche from other parts of pre-war Poland like Volhynia
and the Baltic coast were moved in and people said it would not
be long before they became the majority. Lodz was going to be as
German as Munich and Berlin and a model city showcasing Nazi
architecture and urban planning.

And the Jews? In December the plan began to leak out—
confinement to one part of town. We know now from the discovery of secret German documents that this was supposed to
be temporary, a way station until Litzmannstadt could be made
Judenrein, entirely "cleansed of Jews." But in fact that day would
be far off. The Lodz ghetto would be the longest-lasting concentration of Jews in all of Nazi-occupied Europe.

By the end of 1939, many local Jews had been deported to work
camps in the Protectorate and tens of thousands had fled into

eastern Poland, now occupied by the Soviets. Others had been shot, or died from the difficult conditions. So our numbers were down perhaps by 30% of the pre-war population. But we were still about 175,000 strong and stunned by the posters in the streets early in 1940 announcing that all Jews would be restricted to an area of barely one and a half square miles.

The Germans selected the worst part of Lodz, where Jews had been forced to live in centuries past, Old Town and the much larger Baluty, recently incorporated into the city. Baluty in particular was disgusting, among the filthiest slums anywhere in Europe. There were no zoning laws so flimsy wooden tenements had been put up alongside warehouses and factories, on crooked, unpaved streets and alleys, with no thought to fire, sanitation, or ventilation. There were neither gutters, nor sewers, nor street-lights. The neighborhood was rife with disease and crime—a nest of drug-dealers, prostitutes, and thieves. By the 1930s some solid working class and even middle class families, including a number of Jews, lived in the district but it still had a terrible reputation. If someone was a low-life, we said he was from Baluty.

The date set for the Jewish community to move there en masse was February 8, 1940, and the Polish and ethnic German residents were scheduled to vacate their houses at the same time. But my family, among the first to be resettled in Baluty, went many weeks before the official transfer. One reason could be that the authorities started with our neighborhood, at the southern end of Lodz (and the furthest from Baluty in the far northeast) and went up the map from there, so it may be that we were part of an early experiment. It might also have been that grandfather Katz's connections with Rumkowski gave us the "opportunity" to obtain the best lodging early, before the flood of Jews arriving later. Yet most likely, I think, was the new regime's need for apartments like ours to accommodate the large influx of Volks-

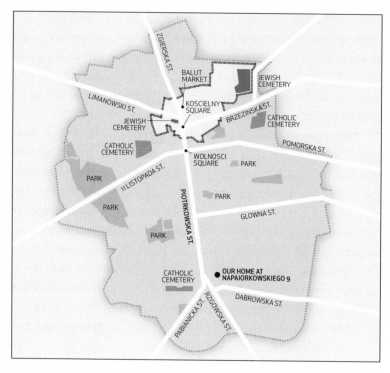

The City of Lodz as of 1939 and the area designated as the ghetto.

deutsche from other parts of Nazi-occupied Europe. Our fine residence, on a good block, in an ethnically German district had to be considered a prime place.

My parents and grandparents were appalled at being uprooted but knew they had no choice and hoped they could return shortly. It was a heavy blow, but maybe, they thought, it would be the last one they'd have to absorb. We were allowed to take household furniture so my father hired a horse-drawn cart (Jews of more modest means would have to push their wagons themselves) and loaded it with two of our beds, linens, and a few other items—including some of his prized religious books. He and my mother put jewelry and cash in their pockets, but hid bulkier valuables in our upstairs apartment. Tateh was required to leave the keys with the building's doorkeeper.

Baluty greeted us with mud and stench. The garbage dumps and excrement pits had not been emptied in months. When we opened the door of our ground floor dwelling on Zydowska Street 34 (now officially Cranachstrasse) our hearts sank even further. It consisted of two small rooms with the plainest wooden furniture: a table, a cot, two chairs and an armoire. The walls were damp, the paint peeling. There was electricity, but only up to 8 pm, and no running water or even a drain; few apartments in Baluty had any indoor plumbing at all. We found a shelf holding several pails to be filled from an old pump down the block. The apartment had a stove, connected with a long heating pipe going to the ceiling, but it had to be fed with coal or wood, which we sensed, quite rightly, would be in short supply. We could warm food on the stove, too, but with fuel such a problem we were

A typically flooded street in the ghetto captured by the noted photographer Mendel Grossman. (courtesy USHMM)

Our apartment on Zydowska Street in the ghetto as it looks today. (The street has been renamed Bojowniko Getta Warszawskiego, Fighters of the Warsaw Ghetto.)

advised instead to cook on a gas-fired burner in a little communal kitchen next door.

It was a bleak picture but before long we realized that our family was among the lucky ones. Including my grandfather, we were four people and most apartments of that size would be filled with more than twice as many—often strangers as well as relatives.

And our dwelling had another advantage: In the floor, we noticed that a trap door opened on a little cellar accessible by ladder. We looked knowingly at one another and immediately covered the area with a velour bedspread we'd brought along. To any intruder it would look like a living room rug.

As Jews left one neighborhood after the other in the late winter and trudged into Baluty it was clear that nourishment was going to be a huge problem. My folks could still afford to buy staples at private stores but many Jews were destitute and almost all unemployed. Food vouchers were distributed by the Gemine, but we all knew its funds would soon run out. After that, it would be every man for himself; we certainly could not depend on the Germans to feed us. In order to stay alive, people would have to sell their valuables for bread.

I wanted my family to have the best possible chance for survival. We had brought along a couple of watches and rings but had also left behind some costly things, a silver serving set among them. So I decided to go back to our abandoned home on Napiorkowskiego and retrieve those possessions. My parents were frantic with worry when they heard my plan but they let me go ahead. I disguised myself as a Polish girl, covering my head with a babushka and my body with one of my mother's loose-fitting wraps. The ghetto wasn't yet sealed—people were still moving in and out of Baluty—and I tried to blend in with the crowds on the streets.

Then I slipped out of the Jewish quarter and hopped on a tramcar heading south. I knew the punishment would be severe if I were caught. My life could end at the age of sixteen. But I kept my composure all the way to Gorny Rynek, trying not to make eye contact with anyone. How my world had completely changed, I thought. Only half a year earlier I was terrified that someone would see me going to the movies on Shabbes.

I didn't enter our upstairs apartment from its private entrance on the street, figuring I might be recognized by a neighbor and that, anyway, the door was probably bolted. Instead I ducked into the building's hallway and walked quickly to our downstairs dwelling. Thankfully, that was unlocked. I went in and bounded up the stairway we'd built to the other unit, still vacant. And there were the items just as we'd left them, hidden between the walls and double-doors that we always left open between the kitchen and living room.

I took a good-sized silver tray and soup ladle and some smaller ladles, and, with string I'd brought along, tied each piece to a belt around my waist; it was the ceremonial *gartel* my father wore to the prayer house, the only waistband any of us had. Mother's wrap now fit more tightly but it was still not obvious that I was a smuggler; it was winter and most people wore bulky clothing. I got on another streetcar back to the ghetto and felt so proud of myself that a few days later I made a second trip back home, for a smaller silver tray and some other utensils. We hid all these valuables in the cellar, and knowing we could use them as barter or a bribe eased our anxiety a bit.

Medicine, though, was often impossible to obtain at any price. By April, my uncle Yankel, whose family had moved to the ghetto about a month after we had, was dying. A diabetic, he lacked enough insulin. Beyond that, he had an infection on his neck and couldn't get the medication to fight it. He passed away on April 22, the first night of Passover. A few days earlier, his daughter Bronka had come to the ghetto to be at his bedside. My older cousin, on her own, had undertaken a brief reconnaissance trip to Warsaw, thinking life might be easier for her family in a city where a ghetto had not yet been established. But the grave illness of her father brought her back. At the end of the Shiva, though, she was trapped along with the rest of us. The Jewish quarter was sealed on the night of April 30 and movement in or out became impossible.

Lodz would be the most impenetrable ghetto in Europe. The Germans demolished all the houses around it, leaving a treacherous no-man's land between the fence and the Aryan side. In contrast with Warsaw, for example, where at least some contact could be made with Polish freedom fighters, once our ghetto was sealed, no food or weapons were smuggled in and virtually

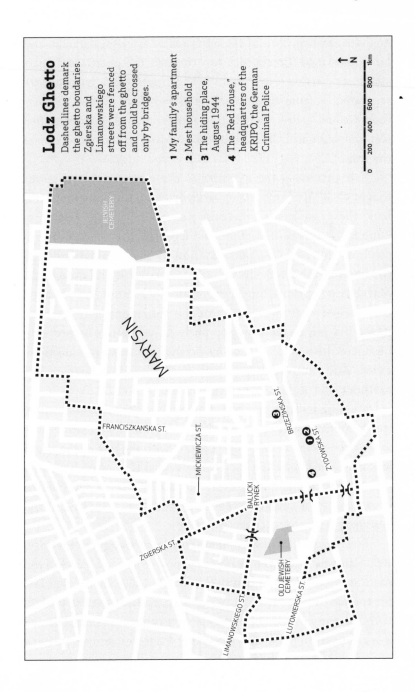

Lodz Ghetto

Dashed lines demark the ghetto boudaries. Zgierska and Limanowskiego streets were fenced off from the ghetto and could be crossed only by bridges.

1 My family's apartment
2 Mest household
3 The hiding place, August 1944
4 The "Red House," headquarters of the KRIPO, the German Criminal Police

N

0   200   400   600   800   1km

JEWISH CEMETERY

MARYSIN

FRANCISZKANSKA ST.

MICKIEWICZA ST.

BRZEZINSKA ST.

❸

❶❷

ZYDOWSKA ST.

❹

BALUCKI RYNEK

ZGIERSKA ST.

LIMANOWSKIEGO ST.

OLD JEWISH CEMETERY

LUTOMIERSKA ST.

no Jews escaped. Two of the city's major arteries, Zgierska and Limanowskiego Streets, did run through the ghetto and their streetcars carried Poles and Volksdeutsche. But barbed wire separated us from these roads, too, and if we needed to cross them we had to use newly built wooden footbridges, twenty-five feet above ground. No measure was spared to separate us from the rest of Lodz.

This extremely tight control is the main reason we never fought back. Although many survivors from my hometown still hang their heads in shame over the lack of armed resistance, I think the special conditions we faced need to be taken into account. The Germans put a station of the criminal police in the heart of the ghetto in the vacated brick parish house of St. Mary's Assumption Church. From the "Red House," as we called that place of incarceration and torture, they monitored our every move. If a Jew so much as approached the ghetto's barbed wire perimeter he would be shot by German sentries, no questions asked. And that was how cousin Bronka's grandfather on her mother's side of the family lost his life.

We were isolated in every conceivable way. Almost no mail, newspapers, or packages were delivered from the outside. There was no telephone or telegraph contact with the rest of the world and from the beginning the Nazis decreed that possession of a radio was a capital crime. Even the lack of sewers deprived us of the route for smugglers and escapees such as existed in the Warsaw ghetto.

Rumkowski saw how vulnerable we were. Caught in this vise, we'd either be starved to death or sent off to a horrible fate in the east. So he struck a unique deal with the Nazis that would last for the next four and a half years: He proposed that the ghetto, with its many industrial buildings and skilled artisans, become a manufacturing hub for Germany. Factories and workshops would churn out war materiel as well as goods for civilians, and in return the entire Jewish community would receive food and be allowed to live.

There was no other way we could survive, he was certain. "Our only path is work," he declared repeatedly. But it meant that Rumkowski constantly had to prove our usefulness to the Nazis. Lacking up-to-date plants or equipment, to say nothing of adequate food or shelter, he had to turn the whole Jewish population into a productive beehive of laborers.

To some extent he succeeded. Under threat of death, we became one of the largest industrial centers of the Reich, operat-

A poster glorifying Rumkowski by the ghetto illustrator Hersch Szylis. (courtesy USHMM)

ing for years after the liquidation of the ghettos of Warsaw, Cracow, Bialystock, and most other cities. In more than a hundred bustling factories, Lodz Jews turned out fur coats and leather goods, caps and gloves, electrical appliances and metal items, furniture and rugs, blankets and quilts, paper and rubber, even corsets and bras. There were also a few cultural events for the workers, a handful of schools for their children, and, for a while, a weekly newspaper. Our ghetto was the only one with its own internal postal system and currency.

Rumkowski reigned over all of this as a kind of king of the Jews, chauffeured around in a fancy black-lacquered droshky. School children staged elaborate shows in his honor and workers presented him with albums of glowing tributes. With much fanfare, the widower married a beautiful woman about half his age and the populace showered the newlyweds with gifts. His portrait hung everywhere and, had the Germans permitted, would have

Rumkowsi speaks in a public square in the ghetto, June 1940. In the background are the spires of St. Mary's Assumption Church in the ghetto. It was used to store the clothing of Jewish deportees. (courtesy USHMM)

Hans Biebow, chief German ghetto administrator, and Rumkowski. (courtesy USHMM)

even graced the ghetto's postage stamps. To him, we were all like children to be kept in line, similar to the waifs in his orphanage. And he dispensed rewards as well as punishment: in the early years we even received a small ration of matzah for Passover.

But of course the ghetto was never the benevolent city-state that the Eldest of the Jews envisioned. Working conditions were atrocious, the pay below subsistence levels, and the atmosphere one of stark terror. The few expressions of dissent—demonstrations, strikes, or even negative talk—were brutally crushed by club-wielding Jewish police.

The Lodz ghetto should really be thought of as an urban slave labor camp and it was highly profitable to the German army and private companies. They simply placed orders with the Nazi overlord, a young businessman named Hans Biebow, and received the finished goods at a cut-rate price. Rumkowski was answerable to Biebow for filling production quotas and dependent on him to feed the hungry, exhausted labor force. In the process, Biebow and his cronies skimmed a fortune for themselves, lived extravagantly, and never showed an ounce of compassion for the tens of thousands of Jews they were working to death.

The inadequate supply of food affected everything in the ghetto and created a new social hierarchy. With few exceptions, ration coupons were distributed only to workers and varied according to the type of labor performed. A skilled worker received a bit more than an unskilled one. The night shift entitled you to extra rations, and foremen and heads of workshops got even more. Near the top of the pyramid were those Jews directly under Rumkowski and his department heads, who managed the ghetto: the commissioners in charge of social welfare, the policemen and firefighters, the judges and court workers. They rarely went hungry.

The privileged layer of society also fattened itself with bribes, resulting in never-ending resentment between the average ghetto dweller and the corrupt higher-ups. Indeed, most Jews suffered a lot at the hands of other Jews—cruel cops, unfeeling bureaucrats, and harsh bosses.

3 Multiple Miracles

FROM THE OUTSET, A SAYING made the rounds of the ghetto: "He who is closest to the pot sticks his fork in first." It was primarily aimed at the greedy big shots, but it also applied to me—quite literally—because my first job was doling out soup in a communal kitchen. Whenever people I knew came up to the counter, I'd dip the long ladle into the bottom of the pail and scoop up as many potatoes and vegetables as I could. Early on, the food was under the kosher supervision of a Chasidic rabbi (a relative of the Gerer rebbe, no less) so I served my own family members often. To be able to give them a little extra sustenance meant the world to me.

I was especially glad to feed grandfather Katz who had suffered a stroke shortly before we were ghettoized. Amidst the turmoil in the fall of 1939, we couldn't take him to the hospital and a neighbor, a midwife, thought she could revive him by pouring hot water on his arms—a common folk remedy in those days—but only succeeded in inflicting serious burns. Naturally, the stress of the ghetto added to his misery and he passed away in October 1940 at the age of seventy-four. Had he died before the war, some of the biggest dignitaries in Lodz would have come to his funeral but all we could manage now was a modest burial and Shiva. He spoke little during that last, greatly diminished year of his life. But I can guess how this man who had worked so hard to benefit his people must have despaired from his sickbed in the ghetto.

Abraham Katz's influence may have been responsible for my employment in the coveted food sector and for the relatively good working conditions of others in my family as well, even as we suffered in many other respects. Although my mother's job, making rugs from strips of old clothes, was nothing special, at least she was not required to labor on Shabbes as were most others. Father was allowed to stay home every day and receive ration coupons anyway; he spent long hours praying and studying with a small group of other Chasidic men and still donned his *shtreimel* and *kapoteh* on the Sabbath and holidays. Aunt Bronka, who traded on her own connections and charm, worked in a grocery store. My cousin Bronka, in her early twenties, probably did the best of all of us, landing a white-collar post in a special factory making fashionable apparel for the wives of Nazi leaders. Biebow, the chief German overseer, was there often and because he didn't want anything to hinder the productivity of this labor department, he treated the expert Jewish tailors and their support staff far better than he did the typical worker. Some of them even enjoyed vacations at a nearby retreat. Bronka's husband, meanwhile, became the manager of a dairy distribution center; that, too, was an enviable post. But of course no Jew, regardless of his or her position, was ever secure.

About half a year into our confinement, a strict ration system was imposed and most of the communal soup kitchens, including mine, were closed. Hunger loomed large as the cold weather of 1940-41 approached, the ghetto's first full winter, but luckily I continued to work dispensing food.

I was assigned to the *Fleischzentralle,* the meat distribution center. With two other girls I labored under the direction of a lecherous boss, a married, middle-aged man, but we were able to fend him off. Many other female workers in the ghetto, though, readily gave in to their supervisors. As conditions worsened, sex became a form of currency. In exchange for extra rations or better living quarters, or simply to hold on to what little they already had, quite a few women who had been virtuous before the war were now willing to do anything. The Germans rarely forced themselves on us sexually; their racism was so extreme that we were usually not seen as objects of desire. But Jewish men in authority frequently did extract sexual favors. Rumkowski himself was known to abuse females, including minors, and he was hardly the only one to commit such acts.

We three shop girls never had to use our bodies for material gain but our way of getting by—shorting the customers—was hardly pure. Of course I'm not proud of our little conspiracy, but I don't know how many people, if they found themselves and their families starving, would have had the moral strength to resist the temptation.

The food we stole was dark red salami made of horses that had dropped dead, plus lots of fillers—the only animal flesh we ever ate in the ghetto. In normal life, I would have been nauseated by this swill but by 1941 I was so famished that it actually tasted good. I knew, too, that it provided much-needed protein. The horsemeat could also be traded on the street for something else, although that carried lots of risk.

But pilfering it wasn't easy. When a shipment came into the

Fleischzentralle we had to account for every ounce both with ration coupons and cash because workers were actually paid a tiny wage in ghetto scrip with which they purchased their food. I was the cashier, noting every transaction in a big ledger book, while the two other girls stood behind the counter and carefully weighed the goods. People waited endlessly for their allotment, a measly quarter-pound a week for most workers, which some gobbled up right in the store. Like other edibles, it was so precious that families often failed to report a death, and postponed a burial, in order to continue to use a corpse's ration. In mid-winter a loved one's dead body might be kept in an unheated house for weeks. Those last coupons were usually the only "inheritance" a child received from his parents.

Our scheme, carried out by the salesgirls with my complicity, was the old "thumb-on-the-scale" trick. Each buyer received just a shade less than he or she was entitled to; the difference was almost imperceptible. But with hundreds of people passing through our shop on the days deliveries arrived, it added up. By the end of the week, we had a couple of pounds left over that we divided three ways. I think the boss suspected our little racket but he never asked to get in on it. I'm sure he had some scam of his own.

The extra horsemeat was a lifesaver because everything else was in such short supply. A year after the establishment of the ghetto, a typical worker's weekly rations, other than the strange salami, consisted of a few pounds of bread and potatoes, less than a pound of beets and cereal, a half pound of flour, and a few ounces each of jam, margarine, and ersatz honey and coffee. Sometimes we got turnips, cabbage, carrots, or rutabagas but they were often rotten. In desperation, people tried to find potato peels, thought to be nutritious, to round out a meal. Eventually potato peels were dispensed only with a doctor's prescription.

It took a lot of self-discipline not to consume all your food in the first few days. By the end of the ration period, which could be a week, ten days, or even two weeks, a loaf of bread—the gold currency of the ghetto—could fetch a fortune on the streets. The bakers' wagons, as they made their way to the distribution centers, were often guarded by police escorts.

Most of the factories supplemented their workers' diets with a mid-day soup, another big advantage of holding a job. Even so, the masses were horribly under-nourished. Years later, I wasn't surprised to learn that the average daily caloric intake in the Lodz ghetto was less than two-thirds of what is needed for a human being to function, let alone perform manual labor. In 1941 7% of the Jewish community starved to death and more than twice that percentage died of hunger the following year. We saw their swollen bodies on the streets, corpses that were thrown onto wagons—usually pulled by people, not horses—and taken to the big Jewish cemetery on the edge of the ghetto.

My growling stomach took over all my waking thoughts and

The photographer, Mendel Grossman, eating with his nephew. (courtesy USHMM)

even invaded my sleep. Every night I dreamt of bread, not fresh, warm bread with butter, but just bread! For nearly all of us, hunger led to fatigue, dizziness, and disease. It often set husband against wife, parents against children. In some cases, hunger drove people insane.

At least my family was blessed with a few sources of additional food. One was my cousin Bronka, whose "plum job" at the Tailor Department entitled her to extra rations. Even though she had a large family of her own to consider, including Debusha, two other sisters, an ailing mother who didn't work, and a very young brother, she sometimes came over to our apartment and generously left us a few of the precious food coupons.

The horsemeat and horse bones I brought home helped as well. My mother sometimes made soup with the bones and she and I devoured that along with the meat. It wasn't kosher, of course, and the learned Chasidic men debated whether or not one was permitted to eat it. Most of them argued that because food was so scarce, horsemeat was allowed because it kept a person alive.

But a few dissented and a consensus was never reached. Of course the Gerer rebbe's ruling would have been the last word, but he was long gone from Poland. And without his permission my pious father would not touch the horsemeat, the only thing I could steal. I'm not sure whether Tateh's understanding of Talmud prohibited it or, rather, that he agreed it was permissible, but simply could not bear to have the repulsive *treyf* meat on his tongue. Either way, while he voiced no objection to my mother or me indulging in horsemeat, he wouldn't go near it.

So I arranged to trade some for a little bread. My two partners in crime had connections with a baker and they were able to make the switch for me. On other occasions they bartered the horsemeat on the black market, and the extra bread was a boon for us all and especially for Tateh. Nevertheless, my father grew thin and weak and I worried about him constantly.

The food crisis in the ghetto deepened even further in the early fall of 1941 with the arrival of tens of thousands of western and central European Jews, many of them highly educated professionals from the great capitals of Berlin, Vienna, and Prague. Some were *Mischlinge,* or part-Jews, and a few had converted to Christianity, not that it counted for anything in the ghetto. The men came off the trains in expensive business suits and neckties, the women in luxurious furs and hats. They were shocked to see our gaunt faces, disheveled clothing, and decrepit dwellings. While we'd been languishing in the ghetto for almost two years, they'd also been living under Nazi rule but at least in their own homes. At first they couldn't believe they'd have to share our fate and we heard that some German Jews thought they'd be put up in hotels. Because of their air of superiority, we despised these *Yekes,* as we called them in Yiddish.

Ultimately they suffered more than we did because they weren't used to the horrendous conditions. But in the short run their Reichsmarks and jewelry bought them some relief. For us the presence of the western Jews led to reduced rations because there were so many more mouths to feed, and it also meant more congested living quarters, hospitals, and workplaces.

Even worse was the spike in black market prices because of the newcomers' buying power. In October the cost of everything on the black market doubled; a loaf of bread went for twelve marks, about half a month's wages for the average factory hand. And the price of food would soar much higher in the months ahead. By late winter people wouldn't part with one of the big round loaves for a hundred marks, and in early spring two hundred. But we could not survive without supplementing our allotted rations. There was no choice but to sell more and more of the family silver and eventually my father had to trade one of mother's diamond rings—for a single loaf of bread. He told us we could always buy diamonds later; for now we had to remain alive.

Being malnourished and also living and working in such close quarters, people were prone to all sorts of disease, and in 1941 tuberculosis swept through the ghetto, infecting thousands. We were also inundated with big, fat lice that turned up in everyone's clothes; you could be talking to someone and suddenly see the bugs crawling across the person's face. It was only a matter of time, we all knew, before we would have to contend with typhus and dysentery as well.

The harsh winter weather took its toll, too. Because we received only meager rations of coal and firewood, people were sometimes found frozen to death in their homes. My parents and I had brought our warm coats—they'd given me a new one, with fur trimming, just before the war—and still we shivered day and night; ice formed on the inside of the apartment's walls and windows. During one cold snap we took the door off the armoire and used it for fuel, and throughout the ghetto, furniture was often chopped up and burned. To get warm, some Jews stole fence posts and outhouse boards, and even carried off banisters and stairs. There were reports of ghetto dwellers awaking to find they had no way to get down from their apartments on higher floors; the wooden stairs had been removed during the night. And yet, as cold as it got inside, the temperature was never low enough to kill the lice. To fight the chill you swaddled yourself, fully dressed, in a wool shawl and a down quilt only to find those items, too, infested with insects.

Suicides occurred almost every day and although it was uncommon in Chasidic circles, one of my cousins did attempt to kill herself by jumping out a window. She survived the fall but many other ghetto dwellers succeeded in taking their own lives by hanging or poisoning themselves, or inviting a bullet by running up to the barbed wire fence. Given the misery of daily life, no one blamed them.

But as the year ended, the biggest threat to our survival was not deprivation—it was deportation. With the influx of the German-speaking Jews, the population was back up to about 165,000—too many to feed and shelter. In December 1941, Rumkowski announced that ten thousand people would have to be "resettled" in the east. He stated that the Nazis had demanded the removal of twice that number but that he had succeeded in negotiating it down. How fortunate, he stated publicly, that he'd also won the right to draw up the list of deportees himself, and that most of those forced to leave would be the "criminal element," people with police records who posed a threat to the peace and security of the ghetto. In fact, many fell into that category simply because they'd been denounced by an informer eager to collect a piece of bread from the police.

The news of the impending deportation led to panic and many likely candidates no longer came to work but went into hiding. Our leader then decreed severe punishment for anyone offering sanctuary to such fugitives, even the doorkeeper of any building in which they were found.

Rumkowski likely knew that by deporting people he was sentencing them to death. This may have been the hidden meaning of a famous line in one of his speeches: "If I were to tell you what I know you would not sleep. So I *alone* am the one who does not sleep." Yet none of the rest of us could say for sure what resettlement meant, what was the actual destination of the trains taking people out of town. At first, a deportee was allowed to sell his furniture and household goods, take with him about thirty pounds of baggage, and change his ghetto scrip (the Rumkys, as we called the banknotes, which were worthless anywhere else) for Reichmarks. So maybe those selected really were being sent to another ghetto or to work the land in the Polish countryside. Indeed, my cousin Hershel actually volunteered for deportation, and he received a whole loaf of bread for doing so. His mother sewed a diamond chain into the seam his coat to help him in his new life.

Others were sure that transfer out of the ghetto led to something terrible, like hard labor in coal mines or stone quarries. I never heard anyone raise the possibility of outright execution, but evacuation from Lodz was usually discussed with such dread, and as something to be avoided at all cost, that some among us may have equated deportation with death. My mother, for example, often wondered aloud what had happened to the people whose clothes came into her rug-making factory. So, with a few exceptions like Hershel, we feared the unknown more than we did the ghetto. Lodz was hellish; to leave it might even be worse.

There was always the chance, too, that if we remained in place, our cage would be opened. Most ghetto dwellers had no news from the battlefield—I did not even know about Pearl Harbor—but we were aware by the second half of 1941 that the Soviet Union was at war with Hitler. Could the Red Army come in and liberate us? Some were so eager to believe salvation was at hand, that if they saw a red warning flag on the rear of a truck, they imagined it was the emblem of Stalin's troops and they started to celebrate.

The initial ten thousand deportees were taken away in groups of about eight hundred a day in January 1942, and as happened so often, the Germans soon raised their demands and Rumkowski felt he had to comply. By the beginning of Passover on April 2, many more people had been marched to the train station—34,000 I later learned. This deportation was aimed primarily at the unemployed; many of them tried to hide, but hunger and cold flushed them out.

The newly arrived western Jews were exempt from that huge wave of expulsion, but as early as May, Rumkowski changed his mind—after all, the doctors, lawyers, and accountants weren't suited for manual labor—so ten thousand of them were removed. Some actually believed the trains would take them back to their cozy homes. By now, the population of the ghetto had been reduced by more than a third of what it was at the end of 1941.

My brother and sister-in-law were deported in March 1942, taken right out of their house by the Jewish police. They lived near us yet I never learned from them or my parents that they'd received the "wedding invitation" as we said in ghetto slang, to report to the authorities, a summons they evidently ignored. But after Moishe and Leah were seized, Mameh and Tateh could no longer spare me the devastating news. We sat around in despair and yet mouthed hopes that their fate might not be too bad.

Years later, other Lodzers confirmed my worst fears. Moishe and his wife were gassed at Chelmno, only forty miles north of the ghetto. Chelmno had been opened at the end of 1941, the first in the vast network of Nazi extermination camps, a crude, though no less lethal, prototype of the more elaborate death factories to come later. Immediately after their arrival, the Jews were forced by SS guards to hand over their valuables and strip off all their clothes. Fifty or more victims at a time were then forced into large, paneled trucks, and asphyxiated with carbon monoxide pumped through a tube from the exhaust pipe. In the same vehicles the bodies were driven to a mass grave in the forest. At first the corpses were dumped in a giant pit but later they were burned in the open air. Until Chelmno closed in the summer of 1944, more than 150,000 people were murdered there, the large majority of them Lodz Jews.

I could not have imagined this in 1942, but I was still terrified that, like Moishe and Leah, my parents would be expelled from the ghetto. Tateh didn't work, putting him in extreme danger of deportation. He and Mameh were around fifty years old and I agonized about how they'd fare on a long, cold journey without me.

By springtime, the ghetto police, desperate to meet their quotas of deportees, rounded up people who had not even received prior notification. I think my parents might have been among them had it not been for the tip-offs we received from Aunt Bronka. Her brains and beauty, and also her *yichus*, or lineage, as a daughter of Abraham Katz, gave her entrée to the central Jewish police station, right across the street from the store where she worked. From the *Sonderkommando*, or Special Jewish Unit, she often learned of deportations a day before they were to take place and would come over to our house before the evening curfew to warn us. Then I'd hide my parents in the cellar with some food and water, close the shutters, padlock the front door of the house, and, when necessary, go in and out through the window. Anyone bent on harming us would think that no one was home.

I smiled with new wisdom when I recalled the Katz family's prewar maxim that "None of the Bronkas are any good" because they'd rebelled and married outside our sect. Well, two Bronkas had already saved my parents and me—we owed our lives to my cousin's ration coupons and my aunt's alarms.

In the summer a bit of stability arrived as the deportations ceased. Food rations returned to levels of the year before and black market prices fell. But now many thousands of Jews from the small towns and villages around Lodz were transported into the ghetto. Among the new arrivals from my father's town of Zdunska Wola were his sister, Miriam, her husband, and seven small children. How I pitied that big Chasidic family, crammed into one little room, the kids screaming for food. And how angry I was at my stupid, selfish uncle who had insisted his wife bear more children even during the war. I visited a few times to help care for the babies but I couldn't see how they'd survive.

With the population on the rise again, we worried there would soon be another mass evacuation. In the meantime, we continued to stretch our limited supply of food as far as it would go. I'll never forget my mother's resourcefulness. She didn't even throw away the used grounds of ersatz coffee; they looked like little oats and she made pancakes out of them, which tasted awful but at least filled us up for a while. And she could make soup even out of grass and leaves.

I was now eighteen and had little leisure after the long hours I put in at the Fleischzentralle and the time I spent caring for my parents. Except for the two Bronkas and Aunt Miriam's family, I had lost contact with my many aunts, uncles, and cousins, including my dear friend Debusha. Most of them lived in different parts of the ghetto, but even more than that, the intense struggle for survival made it hard to think of anyone other than Mameh, Tateh, and myself.

But I did have a few close friends, young people who lived nearby, with whom I passed a couple of enjoyable hours almost every evening. My new companions were very different from the religious kids I'd known before the war. They were not Chasidim and were only partially observant—and with their broad interests they opened a window on a new world for me.

It all began when I met Cesia Mest, a lively girl a couple of years older than me, who lived only two doors down from us with her working-class family, residents in Baluty before it became the ghetto. They had been allowed to stay in their prewar home, and retain all of their furniture, although one of their rooms was requisitioned by the authorities and converted into the gas-fired cooking station for the whole block.

Cesia and I quickly took a liking to one another and I soon met her brother Wolf, eight years my senior, whom everyone called Vevik. He worked as a barber in the family's nearby shop, which remained open during the ghetto's first year and served as a meeting place for Jewish youths from the surrounding streets. One friend was the handsome, fun-loving Feliks Lubka, a policeman assigned to a ghetto streetcar, who became Cesia's boyfriend. Vevik befriended me and later we became much more than friends. But even by 1941, we were a tight-knit foursome—Feliks and Cesia, her brother Vevik and I. Together in the evening, we read aloud passages from Polish novels, sang popular songs and, at least for a while, tried to divert our attention from our wretched circumstances. As hungry, weary, and cold as were, just being together raised our spirits.

We always gathered at the Mest apartment because my

Teenagers in the ghetto only a few blocks from where we lived.
(Photographer Mendel Grossman, courtesy USHMM)

parents were unhappy about my new set of friends. I'm sure they often thought that if it hadn't been for the war, I would have been married to my cousin and perhaps already pregnant. Even though everything else in our lives had been turned topsy-turvy, my parents remained unwavering Gerer Chasidim and didn't want me to go off track and associate with a bunch of non-Chasidic *yings*.

By now, though, I was no longer a child desperate for their approval, but rather a young working woman. The time I spent with my friends was my only pleasure, the only shred of a normal youth I had, and like everyone else in the ghetto, I knew that death could be right around the corner. So despite my parents' objections I continued to go to Cesia and Vevik's at night, an emotional outlet I needed for my very sanity.

But the fragile existence I'd managed to create for myself was jeopardized by a shocking event in late August 1942. Rumkowski decided to crack down hard on the "parasitic" black market, and my two young co-workers were caught trading horsemeat for bread to an undercover Jewish cop. They were arrested and no one ever heard from them again; they must have been shot or dispatched to Chelmno. But first, probably in the course of a brutal interrogation, they gave out my name, telling the investigators they had been illegally bartering stolen food in the street not only for their own benefit, but also for mine. For all I knew, they also revealed the little trick with the scales.

A policeman came to my door and arrested me in front of my horrified parents. Luckily, I was held in jail only a few hours and released on my own recognizance. But I was ordered to stand trial a few days later. No legal counsel was permitted; my fate would be determined by a judge and two jurors.

I went into a tailspin of dread and depression. Would I be imprisoned, tortured, deported, or even executed? There were sometimes public hangings of Jews in the main square when Rumkowski wanted to make an example of a criminal. And if I were gone, how would my parents survive without the extra food I sometimes brought home, and without my help in an emergency? I told Mameh, and Tateh and later Cesia, Vevik, and Feliks of my plight but there was nothing any of them could do. I went to Aunt Bronka, who listened with grave concern and promised to try to help, but influencing the criminal justice system was a tall order even for an insider like her.

On the night of the trial (the proceedings were held in the evening because the jurors and even the judge held regular factory jobs during the day) I was so tense I could barely think straight. No visitors were allowed. I had to face this ordeal utterly alone.

As soon as I walked into the dimly lit courtroom, the walls bare except for Rumkowski's portrait looking down on us, I realized this was summary justice at its worst. I was one of a long line of defendants, each granted only fifteen minutes in front of the bench. Three months in jail was a typical punishment for offenses as slight as stealing a spool of thread from the tailor factory or a stick of wood from the carpentry workshop. I could only wonder what the food rations would be behind bars. And the court had the power to impose far worse penalties, all the way to the death sentence.

I could tell the tribunal had little training in the law and even less knowledge of human nature; clearly they'd gotten their posts solely because of their loyalty to Rumkowski. When it was my turn, I was not read the charges, not permitted to defend myself, or even asked to plead guilty or not guilty. The only reason for my presence was to hear the sentence and then likely be led off in handcuffs.

While I stood there, the three people deciding my fate

fumbled with papers and openly discussed my case.

"Let's assign her to the shit-wagons," said one.

This was the pitiful fecal crew, sad souls made to empty the outhouses of excrement and push it on carts all the way to a dump at the edge of the ghetto. The bumpy streets often caused some of the contents to spill, so you could trace their route by the putrid trail they left behind.

"Yes," said another, "and let's make sure she's at the back of the wagon, where it stinks the most." I was shattered knowing that most of the fecalists contracted typhus and within a few weeks died from it.

The three judges then murmured amongst themselves for a while and finally the magistrate pronounced the penalty: a month's imprisonment. Thank God! It would be a high price to pay but might not prove fatal to me or my parents. Just as I exhaled with relief, the news got infinitely better: "Suspended

Female Fecalist in front of an excrement wagon.
(Photographer, Mendel Grossman, courtesy USHMM)

sentence," declared the judge, "By order of the Eldest of the Jews, Mordecai Chaim Rumkowski, the felon Chava Gerszt is freed because the High Holidays are drawing near."

I ran all the way home, threw myself into the arms of my parents, and then went over to the Mests to share my joy with them. The judges and jurors were notoriously bribable but Aunt Bronka would never tell me if she'd arranged to *shmier* them, literally smear their palms, as we called under-the-table payments in Yiddish. And if so, why did they think they had to scare me half to death with talk of the fecal wagons? Did Rumkowski himself intervene to help me? He had certainly not lifted a finger for my brother and sister-in-law a few months earlier. I learned later that others, too, had been pardoned due to the approaching holidays. But it was not a blanket order because not everyone convicted of stealing and bartering food was spared. Why I was let off, I'll never know.

Yet I didn't emerge from the courtroom completely unscathed. I was not allowed to return to the Fleischzentrale or work around food anymore; my new assignment was a ten-hour shift in a noisy, crowded factory, stripping and sorting scraps of leather all day. In the *Trennabteilung*, as it was known, I sorely missed the extra horsemeat my old job generated, to say nothing of the camaraderie I felt toward the other two girls.

But the worst thing was that I now had a criminal record making it much more likely that I'd be a target of the police during the next deportation. And that meant Mameh and Tateh were even more vulnerable than before. They could easily be picked up if the cops came to our house looking for me. Aunt Bronka's warnings of future raids became more vital than ever. In periods of danger, I'd hide my parents in the cellar and, for my own safety, spend the night in her apartment.

But even Aunt Bronka could not protect us from the sweeps

of early September 1942, the cruelest deportations in the ghetto's entire history. It began early on the first day of the month, the third anniversary of the outbreak of the war, when half a dozen trucks ominously pulled up in front of the ghetto's largest hospital. All the patients were seized—including the children and elderly, those who could walk and those who couldn't. Jewish police pulled people out of their sickbeds, and interrupted surgeries in progress.

Even more vicious were the Germans. Despite everything in the past three years, we were shocked by their savagery now. They fired point-blank at patients, doctors, and nurses who didn't move quickly enough, and threw people, wrapped in bandages and hospital linens, out of four-story windows to their deaths below. Rumkowski may not have known in advance about this *Aktion*; two of his own relatives were in the hospital (to get a bed there required connections) and they were seized like everyone else. Over the next few days, those who had succeeded in fleeing the infirmary, as well as other sick and injured Jews throughout the ghetto, were picked up as well. The message was clear: Anybody who couldn't work would be sent away.

What did this policy mean for the ghetto's children? Those ten and over were required to toil in the factories and were therefore useful to the regime, but rumors flew that the younger kids were expendable. Yet many parents refused to believe such talk, insisting that even the Nazis could not be so inhumane as to separate the little ones from their mothers and fathers.

On September 4 the Eldest of the Jews addressed the crisis. More than a thousand ghetto dwellers gathered around as he mounted a makeshift stage in a large square in front of the firehouse. I wasn't there but soon heard about what he said. No one in the ghetto spoke of anything else.

We'd all expected Rumkowski would try to calm us by forcefully denouncing the "rumor-mongers" as he had many times in the past. Instead he wept like a little boy and told us the ghetto children would indeed have to be sacrificed. He began by relaying to us the German demand for twenty thousand more Jews: all the elderly, the ill, *and children under ten*. Rumkowski, himself childless, declared it was necessary to give them up in order to save the rest of us, the eighty to ninety thousand who would be left: "I must perform this difficult and bloody operation—I must cut off limbs in order to save the body itself... Give into my hands the victims so that we can avoid having further victims."

He claimed that he'd been able to reduce the number from the original ultimatum of twenty-four thousand, but gone was his usual bravado. "A broken Jew stands before you," he wailed, "I understand you mothers; I see your tears, all right... I suffer because of your anguish, and I don't know how I'll survive this—where I'll find the strength." Yet even at this point he didn't doubt that his strategy was correct. A man in the crowd shouted out that each family should be left with at least one child but Rumkowski would not be budged. "Brothers and sisters, hand them over to me!" he insisted, "Fathers and mothers, give me your children!"

His remarks were followed by hysteria throughout the ghetto. Parents wracked their brains to figure out where to hide their offspring but by now we all knew that basements, attics, and outhouses were the first places the beasts would search. Others vowed they would never release their kids to a stranger, even on pain of death. Still others talked of killing their children themselves in order to spare them the horrors that lay ahead. But there were optimists among us still: people who said the youngsters would be safe, that the Germans were preparing a large children's home to be run by Rumkowski, a former orphanage director.

*A Jewish policeman guards a group of children rounded
up during the Gehsperre. (courtesy USHMM)*

The next day the ghetto was put under a twenty-four hour
general curfew for a week, *Gehsperre*, the Nazis called it. And
the roundup began. It was conducted by the Jewish police, fire
fighters, and truck drivers; they received triple rations of bread,
horsemeat, and sugar, and their own children were exempted
from the decree. But like the raid on the hospital, German soldiers took part as well, often entering homes, dragging people
out by the neck, and shooting them on the spot. I saw many of
the dead lying in the streets, and historians later estimated that
six hundred Jews were killed in the ghetto that week in addition
to the nearly twenty thousand deported. I heard mothers screaming the names of children literally torn from their breasts.

This was a new stage of terror. The killers held lists of residents
and addresses and, with ferocious dogs, went house to house,
assembling all the inhabitants for selection in the courtyard of
their apartment block. It made no sense to move my parents to

This classic photo by Mendel Grossman shows a child selected for deportation being bid farewell by his family on the opposite side of a wire fence. (courtesy USHMM)

the cellar, I realized. The dwelling of anyone unaccounted for was ripped apart and a person caught in hiding was executed then and there.

I also had reason to hope my folks would pass the inspection. They were not in the category of elderly (over sixty-five) and although far from healthy, weren't as feeble as many others; they were not *Musselmaenner*, or Moslems, the term used in the ghetto as well as the death camps to refer to people who walked around like zombies with yellowish skin. Still, I rubbed their cheeks as hard as I could to get more color into their faces. And I tried something else that might give us an advantage. Even though I no longer worked at the Fleischzentralle, I had never turned in my white armband designating me as a municipal worker. I slipped it on now. And then we went outside to learn our fate.

I was evaluated first and told by a German officer that I could remain in the ghetto, hardly a foregone conclusion given my prior criminal conviction. But a moment later he made a dismissive motion with his hand and a soldier shoved both my parents toward the aged and children. I couldn't stop myself from shrieking even though I'd just seen Jews get their teeth knocked out for less.

My outburst didn't cause any harm but neither did it do any good. Right before my eyes, Mameh and Tateh were prodded with rifle butts onto a big flatbed truck. Its engine started up and it began to roll!

By now my screams had become sobs and a big, beefy Gestapo man named Schmidt came over to me and asked something that ought to have been obvious: *Warum weinst du?* he wanted to know, "Why are you crying?"

"Because my parents are on that transport," I stammered in German.

Incredibly, his small blue eyes revealed a twinge of compassion: "Well, tell the Jewish police I said to let them go."

I could hardly believe it, but I turned on my heels and started running after the vehicle, surrounded by a cordon of cops and making its way through the narrow ghetto streets. It was pandemonium as dogs barked, gunshots went off, and people fell dead, but I tried to tune out all of that and focus only on my parents. When I caught up with the truck, and breathlessly told a Jewish officer of the reprieve my parents had been given, he looked at me like I was an idiot and raised his rubber club.

I raced back to Schmidt and explained what had happened. Once again he amazed me: He took a pencil and pad from his pocket and wrote a note authorizing my parents' release. I thanked him in the most formal and flowery German I could muster, and, clutching the piece of paper, began the second, much longer run to the truck.

I approached the same cop, fell to my knees, kissed his hand, and showed him the message. He was not impressed. "You could have written that yourself," he said, "Get lost before I beat the crap out of you."

Now there was nothing to do but rush back to our courtyard and hope that Schmidt was still there. He was just completing his day's "work" but gave me yet another minute of his time. As I related the latest rebuff, his face began to show anger toward the Jewish policeman and I realized that stronger than any sympathy he may have had, was the issue of authority. I beseeched him with the utmost care: "*Sehr geehrter Herr Offizier,* might it perhaps be possible for me to receive something official from you proving the authenticity of your order?" He nodded, and with a rubber stamp he pulled out of a little leather bag, validated the note.

"Let's see what kind of rotten Jew doesn't acknowledge this," he thundered.

Yet again, in a language I hated to speak, the deepest gratitude flowed from my lips. And once more I set out for the truck, running as far and fast as my weak body could carry me. By now the vehicle had left the ghetto proper and was in outlying Marysin, approaching the Radegast railway station, the transit point to the camps. Rain had started falling making the cobblestones slippery and my rescue mission even harder.

Soaked and on my last legs, I finally found my parents under guard in a kind of barrack, huddled with hundreds of other Jews awaiting the next train. But this time I had a stamped note in my hand and it made all the difference. With Mameh and Tateh at my side, I walked out of that warehouse of doomed human beings.

Even with the free pass, we tried not to be noticed as we made our way back to the little apartment on Zydowska Street. After all, we had no right to be out on the streets during a general curfew. But now the rain and dark skies were our allies and we were barely seen. Once we closed the door, we dried off, hugged one another tightly, and rejoiced in our good fortune. Yet within minutes my body fell apart from the severe mental and physical stress I'd been under for many hours.

It began with flu-like symptoms (influenza was common in the ghetto) but I soon became much worse with stomach cramps, terrible fatigue, and high fever. A physician came to our apartment—he wore two yellow stars like every other Jew—but he had no medications in his little black bag except for some aspirin and distilled water, so there was little he could provide beyond the diagnosis. I had typhus, he told my frantic parents. I found out later that almost a thousand cases were reported in 1942 alone, and countless others went unrecorded because many of those stricken didn't see a doctor even once.

Was it any wonder the infested ghetto was plagued by this ailment? The main transmitters of the typhus epidemic were vermin such as body lice and bedbugs and they were everywhere. Beyond that, the few vegetables we got were often caked in dirt and not washed properly by weary workers who sometimes couldn't obtain hot water. It was also hard to clean one's clothes; even when we were issued soap with our rations it never seemed to do the job. Bad nutrition and long work shifts weakened our immune systems and the intense summer heat and winter cold made us even more susceptible.

Normally, I would have been quarantined, but that was impossible since the entire hospital system had been dismantled during the *Shperre* (as we referred in Yiddish to the big roundup and curfew) and most of the employees of the Department of Health had been dismissed. In fact, when the Gestapo raided the infirmaries, some people with contagious diseases went into hiding throughout the ghetto, further spreading the sickness.

My parents were lucky in one respect: I never infected either of them. Most ghetto apartments were much more congested and easily became incubators of the bacteria.

Typhoid fever, a different disease from typhus, ravished us, too, due to the lack of any real sanitation system. Because human excrement was simply loaded onto wagons, pushed through the streets, and dumped in open pits, infected fecal matter often polluted the well water. The biggest killer among the infectious diseases, however, was tuberculosis; it spread rapidly in the over-crowded factories.

Unlike TB, typhus was usually not fatal. But my case did turn out to be life threatening and eventually I lost conscious-ness. While in a coma I contracted pneumonia and before long suffered from dysentery as well, yet another widespread illness in the ghetto resulting from contaminated food and water. In addition to all my other symptoms, I now had bloody diarrhea. Worst of all was the inflammation of my gall bladder, which soon followed. The pain was unbearable and I screamed in agony.

I was bedridden for two months. Mameh had to go work and bolted the door when she left because my father and I were prime candidates for deportation—an older, unemployed religious man and a once-healthy young worker, now deathly ill, and with a criminal record to boot.

Tateh, meanwhile, did everything he could to bring me back to health. Mother was the one who changed my soiled, sweat-soaked nightgown and washed me—modesty prevailed even in the midst of this crisis—but he sat by my bedside day and night. I was so weak that I couldn't even stand without his help.

He bartered his own meager rations to get what I needed to survive. First he obtained some pure water and every hour put drops into my mouth. Then he got sago, a powdery starch similar to tapioca, sometimes used in the ghetto to thicken soup. That helped bind me up and eased the diarrhea.

It had to be dangerous and difficult for him to trade for these items on the street. Rumkowski cracked down on the Chasidic community after the Shperre, allegedly for reasons of health and cleanliness, and prohibited beards and long black clothing. Father, though, wouldn't shave or dress differently and was vulnerable as soon as he walked out the door. He carried a sack of potatoes to barter; they were his main source of nutrition yet now he was ready to part with them.

One day he brought home something that I knew cost a lot more than potatoes—liquid opium—which I desperately needed as a painkiller for my gall bladder infection. I never learned how he got it. Desired by Germans as well as Jews, the healthy as well as the sick, opium was almost always lacking. Even with a doctor's prescription, people had to wait the whole day at the pharmacy just to find out if any medication was available and my father's traditional garb precluded him from standing in line. He must have procured it on the black market although I don't know of any valuables that we still had left to trade. Maybe he had squirreled away one last heirloom for just such an emergency.

The drug did its work—I wish that more ghetto inhabitants could have experienced that relief—and the stabbing abdominal pains ceased. But more wondrous was my recovery from typhus, pneumonia, and dysentery. Within two months I was able to get out of bed and walk on my own; by late November I went back to work at the factory.

All three of us were still alive, but it had taken multiple miracles. With the next winter upon us and the occupiers growing ever more barbaric, I seriously doubted we'd live to see the war's end.

4 Impossible Choices

IN CLOSE FAMILIES LIKE MINE, when one person fell ill, often a parent, child, or spouse would work extra hours or stint on food, and then soon become sick too. "You save someone else at the price of yourself" was frequently heard.

Even before I was stricken, my father had been wasting away, partly because he refused to eat the unkosher meat we were issued. Giving up his potatoes, and probably more, to keep me alive pushed him over the brink into starvation. That he died for me is something I've had to live with the rest of my life.

He became progressively weaker during the frigid winter of 1942-43, as temperatures dipped below freezing in our apartment. By late January came the telltale signs: sunken cheeks creating an "hourglass" face, swelling of the hands, feet, and eyelids, and glistening, wide-open eyes. All the energy left his body and he could barely move. Few Americans have seen a person die of hunger. I witnessed it many times in the ghetto and that winter watched my own father slowly starve to death.

The doctor, aware of the bitter irony of his words, told us father needed to eat better. But it was too late now to feed him extra potatoes or vegetables even if we could get them. He required a special liquid mixture of nutrients, vitamins, and electrolytes—impossible to obtain for any price. Milk might have helped, but even that was not to be found.

I tried to freshen him up as best I could, combing his beard and shifting his position in bed. Even with all the shortages, a low grade of tobacco was included in the rations and sometimes I'd roll him a cigarette, using a little machine he'd brought from home. That gave him an ounce of pleasure; in those days we didn't understand the dangers of smoking even for someone who was critically ill.

I also made another mistake: I fetched water from the communal pump in order to wash the lice off his face but I didn't realize how cold it would be. The water froze on his skin and probably added to his respiratory problems. Before long he caught pneumonia.

Near the end, a doctor recommended strychnine to stimulate his heart. It was a Friday, March 13, 1943, and I took off work—always a risky act—to spend the day waiting at the pharmacy. Luckily, the drug was available and before Shabbes I headed home with a glimmer of hope.

But nearing our apartment I noticed a lot of religious men milling about. Gripped with fear, I opened the door and saw the black coats encircling his bed. It will soon be the Sabbath, I was told; the funeral will be held on Sunday.

All my life I'd recited the *Sh'ma* several times a day but now—with all my heart, with all my soul, with all my might—I cursed God. I screamed it to the heavens and didn't care who heard me. Years later my anger would turn to non-belief. But as

I stood staring at Tateh's lifeless body, I knew that the faith of my youth had crumbled forever. I lost it in the same instant that I lost my father.

Of course I had witnessed horror after horror for three and a half years. But for Tateh, of all people, to die that way, extinguished something that could never be rekindled. I knew better than anyone how his whole life had been in the service of God, even to the point of foregoing the horsemeat I'd brought home the year before. But more than that was the goodness he showed people, not only me whose life he had just saved, but also complete strangers whom he helped with one *mitzvah* after another. What possible divine plan could be served by this saintly man's agonizing, senseless death at the age of fifty-two? And what had any of us Jews done to deserve this nightmarish imprisonment in our hometown?

The Chasidim methodically washed my father's body according to Jewish law and wrapped him in a traditional burial shroud. In normal times he would have been removed to a mortuary but these were not normal times. His corpse remained in the apartment with mother and me for the next day and a half. Mameh sobbed quietly and barely uttered a word.

Tateh was buried in the huge Jewish cemetery in the ghetto's northeastern reaches, past the open fields of Marysin, barren at winter's end. During the long procession there, the plain wooden box holding his remains was pulled on a cart by men with whom he had prayed and studied over the years, although most of his *chevra*, or fellowship group, was already gone by 1943. I comforted my mother as we walked behind the "hearse," but more often I was alone with my thoughts about Tateh who had doted on me from the time I was a toddler.

I watched the gravediggers move sluggishly. Hungry and overworked like everyone else in the ghetto, they buried dozens of bodies every day. We received a slip of paper indicating the location of father's plot but I also made my own mental note of exactly where he lay in relationship to fixed landmarks like the brick wall and entrance to the cemetery. If I survive, I promised myself with my fists clenched, I will return here one day and erect a proper tombstone. For now, all I could place on the mound of earth was a small tin nameplate that I'd been handed by a cemetery worker.

Ten men regularly came over to our apartment to say prayers during the shiva. But otherwise Mameh and I had no visitors. We sat alone for the week.

All of my protective instincts were now turned toward my mother. Soon after Tateh's death she developed a serious sickness of her own—rickets, or softening of the bones. This condition too was common in the ghetto and those afflicted were called *katshkes*, or ducks, because the decalcification caused people to waddle. It became part of the ghetto's famous gallows humor: "We used to eat ducks and walk like horses; now we eat horses and walk like ducks."

Rickets resulted from a deficiency of calcium and vitamin D. Most people in the ghetto, Mameh included, worked in a factory all day and then returned home exhausted; they rarely got any sun. Even so, with a more balanced diet she could have quickly recovered. Cod liver oil or even butter would have helped, but both were phenomenally expensive. So my mother remained racked by this disease in 1943 and 1944, suffering severe leg pains. Her bones were actually soft to the touch and still she went to work.

There was one remedy, however, for those fortunate enough to obtain it. Vigantol, essentially a concentrated dose of Vitamin D, was dispensed with a doctor's prescription in vials of 10 cubic centimeters. Early on, it was allowed only for young children who desperately needed to make up for the shortage of milk. Later, with most of the kids gone, it was permitted for adults yet pharmacies rarely had enough to go around. Like everything else, it could be obtained on the black market but fetched sky-high prices. A kind of "Vigantol craze" developed with speculators accumulating it and driving up rates from 35 to 300 marks by the spring of 1944. The astronomical cost of Vigantol made people think it could work wonders and tall tales about its effectiveness caused prices to spike even further. Many sold everything they had to get the tonic, convinced it could cure not only rickets, but other diseases as well.

I could not compete in a bidding war for the Vigantol mother needed so I had to stand in line like all the other common folk. Once when I heard a shipment was due to arrive I got there at dawn and had to wait until nightfall the next day—thirty-six hours—to get the magic potion. Latecomers naturally tried to cut in front of me but I held my ground.

Vigantol helped for awhile but, like the rest of us, my mother was tormented by hunger. By the winter of 1943-44 even our pitifully low food rations were frequently disrupted. Vegetables often arrived frozen and inedible, and bread and potatoes sometimes failed to show up at all. Meat, even the vile horsemeat, was now just a memory. And when a food shipment did reach the ghetto it was "skimmed" by the higher-ups—for their own consumption or to sell on the black market—and we workers saw but a portion of it. In late January 1944, we received only a few pounds of grain, radishes, and carrots—to last for fourteen days. The mid-day soup at one's workplace was now a matter of life and death but that too was being watered down. In an echo of the Vigantol frenzy, people thought they could be invigorated by potato peels, selling on the street for 60 marks a kilogram. A common dish made out of potato peels and ersatz coffee grounds was called *babka*, or ghetto "cake."

By springtime, as they had in prior years, some ghetto dwellers obtained seeds from the authorities and planted their own vegetables. Even a single slender onion stalk, grown in a window box, was a valuable commodity. One man filled a baby carriage with soil, creating a mobile vegetable patch. Anything planted outside, of course, was likely to be uprooted by thieves even though the "gardens" were protected with fences made of rusted old bedsteads. In 1944, the ghetto was picked clean of every living thing except for some of the bigwigs' fruit trees and vegetable plots in Marysin, and they were guarded around the clock. I don't even remember seeing a dog or cat. People even pulled up and ate the few blades of grass between the cobblestones.

Bread was of course the greatest delicacy. We often made it expand by putting it in soup. But however you ate it, you needed tremendous self-discipline not to consume your entire loaf in the first few days, something I did all too often. My mother, though, meticulously allotted herself a daily portion and never exceeded it. The two of us pooled items like flour, sugar, and vegetables, but bread was in a different category, kept in separate compartments, and toward the end of a ration period she still had some when I usually didn't.

During one of those times, I came home from work earlier than Mameh and grew obsessed with a quarter loaf I knew she still had. That it was stale and maybe a bit moldy meant nothing— it was still bread. I could never ask her to share it because we both knew she needed it more than I did. And she was the one with the foresight and will power to have set it aside.

But there it was, staring at me, while the knot in my stomach grew tighter. I agonized about it and resisted for a long time, but the moment came when I couldn't stop myself. I put her bread on the table and with our sharp Shabbes knife, cut off a thin slice and scarfed it up.

She won't notice it, I told myself, but immediately felt terrible about what I'd done. I feel guilty about it today, nearly a lifetime later. I'd stolen bread from my sick mother! Others behaved the same way or even worse toward their loved ones. There was no clearer sign to me that the Germans had broken our spirits as well as our bodies.

If there was one thing I craved as much as bread it was shoes. The rough cobblestone streets had worn down the soles of the pair I'd had when I'd entered the ghetto and anyway I'd outgrown them and had to cut off the tips. Now my toes poked out, exposed to filth and frost. Many others wore wooden clogs with canvas tops made out of used knapsacks; I didn't see that as much of an improvement.

By late fall of 1943, with winter on its way, I was ready to do anything for decent shoes. I knew that to buy a pair on the black market would cost about 500 marks; that might as well have been a million dollars. But after work I'd loiter in front of the Leather and Saddlers' Labor Department on the slim hope that someone might take pity on me. Also hanging around there was a middle-aged cobbler who had extra shoes but was seeking leather to repair others. When he told me his situation, I offered to provide him leather scraps from the *Trennabteilung*, the factory where I tore apart, sorted, and bundled parts of German uniforms, and we had a deal.

The tough Jewish foremen watched us carefully and I knew that to pilfer pieces of leather was a capital crime. This was not like stealing horsemeat; the uniforms coming through my busy factory were *Wehrmacht* property and any theft was considered sabotage. Indeed, a month earlier a leather and saddlery worker

A workshop in the Leather and Saddlers' Labor Department. (courtesy USHMM)

had been caught swiping some material and was hanged in public for his offense. The poor guy's fellow workers were made to watch the execution, as were his wife and two children.

But going without a pair of good shoes also carried a lot of risk. I could step on something sharp or contaminated and get an infection, which I'd be unable to treat; I could get frostbite in winter and be unable to work.

So, very cautiously, I lifted small fragments of leather, only a few square inches each, concealed them in my palm, then under my clothing, and later, in the factory's outhouse, hid them in my underwear before walking home. Even the girls at my worktable, only inches away, never suspected I'd snatched anything. The leather had been on pants and collars, but since I immediately ripped the uniforms into pieces, my robbery would be hard to trace in the factory. Of course there was a growing pile of scraps in our apartment, but I hid that away in the cellar.

Finally the big day came. The shoemaker and I each carried the goods in a plain sack and quickly made the exchange on the street. I was thrilled with my "purchase"—sturdy, nearly new shoes, with strong laces, that came up over the ankle. They were like diamonds, worth more to me than all of my other possessions combined; I wore them throughout the rest of my days in the ghetto.

Where had those shoes come from? Had they belonged to a respectable Jew from Vienna, say, who, had been transferred to our ghetto and suddenly needed to trade them for food? Had they once been owned by someone rounded up and resettled in the east? I didn't know and I didn't care. All that mattered was that my feet were now protected.

Through all of this, I tried several times a week to visit my three dear friends—Cesia Mest, her boyfriend, Feliks Lubka, and her brother, Vevik. The Mest family would experience a tragedy of its own: in early 1944, Cesia and Vevik's older brother, Alex, received a notice to report for "labor outside the ghetto." He was on a list of about 1,700 workers to be evacuated and although only young men were targeted, it was by far the largest resettlement since the *Shperre* a year and a half earlier, and reminded many of that roundup from which no one had returned.

Some of the designated men went into hiding but Alex was able to avoid resettlement another way: He paid someone else to go in his place, an alternative acceptable both to the Jewish police and the Germans, who simply wanted to reduce the ghetto's population. The going rate was two loaves of bread plus a half-pound of margarine or marmalade and some sugar. It meant that the replacement could eat his fill and still have something left over—a tempting offer in the desolate winter of 1944.

How Alex accumulated all that food, I never learned. By then, a loaf of bread went for about two hundred marks if you could find one at all. But he succeeded and, in effect, bought his life. We cared deeply about Alex and didn't even know his replacement so we were overjoyed.

The substitute kept his part of the bargain and reported for "duty" but so many others on the list failed to show up or to engage substitutes that the 1,700-man quota remained unfilled for weeks. Alex's name was reinstated and this time he couldn't buy his way out. The Jewish police picked him up and kept him for a few days in a detention center where we were allowed to visit him. Then they put Alex on a train and none of us ever heard from him again.

So there were times when I tried to comfort the Mests just as they and Feliks consoled me after my father died. But usually we didn't dwell on our sorrows; we tried to carve out an island of calm in an ocean of insanity. The Mests' mother was always home when I came over, but we four young people congregated at one end of a long table and were hardly aware of her presence. There was often laughter when we were together; everywhere else I was surrounded only by sadness.

I drew closer to my companions after Tateh died. He had known merely that Cesia and I were friends, exchanging books, and that Vevik was her brother. While I couldn't bear to hurt father by getting too involved in a non-religious circle, his passing released me from that concern. At the same time, his death naturally left me enraged, lonely, and depressed; I needed my friends' companionship more than ever. And now that I had turned away from God, and no longer prayed or read the Bible, my outlook and behavior was identical to theirs: We were proud of being Jewish, but not inclined to practice Judaism.

Most important was the tenderness I was developing toward Vevik. At first, he had just been a friend. By 1943, he was delighting me with his wit and impressing me with his intelligence, and I wanted to be with him every chance I could. I was nineteen and he, at twenty-seven, seemed quite mature and fully at home in the modern, secular world I was entering. He was a working class guy—a former barber and now a factory worker—but also knowledgeable about the great Polish authors and composers. He had a lot to teach me.

We would hold hands, the first time I'd ever touched a male outside my family. And then we'd sneak out to one of the seldom-used passageways connecting the compound to share caresses and to kiss. It may not sound like much from the standpoint of twenty-first century America, but given my sheltered background it was electrifying. Vevik was my first love. He reached my mind, body, and soul.

In the spring of 1944 we decided to get married. Although the rabbinate had been abolished after the Shperre, Rumkowski himself performed about a dozen weddings almost every Sunday evening, one after the other, in a Marysin auditorium. On April

Rumkowski signing a wedding certificate. (courtesy USHMM)

23, we were one of those couples. My memory of the wedding has faded over the years but I know it was not a joyous occasion; there was no *chuppah*, no breaking of a glass, no white dress, and not even wedding rings. I don't believe any of our friends or relatives attended. Even so, the ceremony included a basic marriage contract and the exchange of something of value, which met the requirements of Jewish law. The marriage was also entered in the municipal records.

We received an entire loaf of bread and some honey from the Eldest, a huge incentive. For some of the couples Rumkowski married, that was the only motivation. But we wed mostly to express our deep commitment to one another, our pledge that if we survived, we'd be husband and wife after the war.

Yet we did not live as husband and wife in the ghetto, which lasted only four months after our wedding. We remained neighbors rather than set up a new household ourselves because the overriding concern for both of us was our frail mothers and we had to focus on their well being. There were precious few opportunities for Vevik and me to be alone.

We also kept our marriage a secret from everyone but Cesia and Feliks lest Mameh find out. I knew she would be devastated if I married a *ying*. Merely my attraction to Vevik, which she sensed despite my attempts to minimize it, sent her into fits of despair.

She stubbornly clung to tradition. Except for eating *treyf* (and even that could be in accordance with Jewish law in this life-or-death situation), she would remain devout to the end, lighting Shabbes candles when she could get them and, even when our table was bare, always saying the blessings. She kept her well-worn prayer book close at hand and recited the *Tillim*, or Psalms, all the time. The deportation of her son and daughter-in-law and horrid death of her husband of thirty-five years made not the slightest dent in her beliefs.

I'm grateful that Judaism gave her comfort and purpose amidst such trauma. But her strict piety also meant that she felt the betrothal to my cousin—arranged by my father and uncle back in 1937—was still binding. "You are still engaged," she reminded me sharply before I slipped out of the house, and, often with tears in her eyes, she'd ask: "Have you forgotten who you are?"

She rightly saw that the core of my identity was changing. I could not stop visiting Vevik, Cesia, and Feliks, despite the pain it caused Mameh. I don't know how I would have survived without those three; I needed them no less than I needed bread and shoes, no less than Mameh needed to *daven*.

So I stayed at my mother's side when she ushered in the Sabbath as I had my whole life. But then I'd leave her for the new world two doors away.

By May 1944 a different mood had come over the ghetto, a sense that Germany was losing and the war ending. But those expectations also brought fresh fears. What further blows would the sadistic monsters inflict on us before the liberation? As the weather got warmer we entered a season of hope and dread like none in the ghetto's history.

No one in my circle knew of the Normandy invasion on June 6, but I learned later that many others in the ghetto did. A few brave souls secretly listened to radios—strictly forbidden to Jews throughout the German occupation—and passed on the news. They were caught and executed but not before they informed thousands not only of D-Day, but also of the plot to kill Hitler on July 20 and the Red Army's advance on Warsaw the following month.

Even though I wasn't aware of those specifics, I could read the faces of Jew and German alike and gather that the Third

Reich's days were numbered. There were more tangible signs too. By June, air raid sirens sounded in Lodz and people talked about spotting Allied planes overhead and hearing Soviet cannon in the distance. Some even put an ear to the ground and, from the reverberations they heard, tried to gauge how far we were from the front. Others were sure that even before the Red Army arrived, the Germans would have to flee in order to defend their homeland; it could happen any day, they said. We didn't put a lot of stock in such "military experts" but it did seem that our ordeal was almost over.

Yet in the meantime we faced great danger. On June 16, we learned from Rumkowski that thousands of men were needed to clear debris from bombed-out German cities like Munich. At first the request was for "voluntary registration" and all sorts of incentives were offered even beyond food and clothing: entire families could travel together, fifteen kilos was allowed for each person, and mail service would be available.

But by now few believed such promises. Figuring that the Soviets might already be at the Vistula, only seventy miles away, most people preferred to stay put. The ghetto had made the greatest sacrifices—even surrendered its children—but now it looked like a significant remnant, about 70,000 by the summer of 1944, might actually survive.

Yet the Germans applied more and more pressure. We heard that the Eldest of the Jews, now sixty-eight, had been severely beaten in his office by chief ghetto administrator Biebow. They had argued furiously in the past, we all knew, but nothing like this had ever happened before. Rumkowski's face and head were so badly bloodied that he had to be hospitalized during the critical weeks of late June. No one knew the exact reason for Biebow's violent outburst, only that it boded ill for all of us. Had a price been demanded of Rumkowski that even he felt was too dear?

Around the same time the call-up for laborers was changed from voluntary to obligatory. 10,000 people must leave the ghetto, the authorities announced, requiring the head of each labor department to compile a list of evacuees. The rewards to report remained in place and the Germans also agreed to pay ten marks to every deportee and also to buy the evacuees' furniture and household goods. If you didn't want to sell your belongings, you also had the option of storing them in a ghetto warehouse.

Thousands complied with this directive; a high proportion were western Jews who thought they'd be heading home as transports carrying around seven hundred and fifty left almost every day in the last half of June. Many other ghetto dwellers went into hiding. It was rumored that the same trains leaving Lodz returned only a few hours later. So how could they have brought passengers deep into Germany? The quick turn-around was reminiscent of the Shperre. Later we learned that the destination of the transports of June 1944 was in fact the same as that of September 1942: the nearby Chelmno death camp.

Neither my mother nor I, nor any of the Mests, nor Feliks was on the lists of deportees. But we watched in horror as the ghetto police hunted down those who had gone underground. Their food rations were terminated, of course, and dire threats were made against anyone harboring fugitives. Still, most of them remained in hiding.

The pursuit continued in July and included midnight raids— "Jews hunting Jews," people said—while the rest of us continued to work in our respective factories. Every day that passed, we figured, was a small victory that brought us closer to liberation. Maybe the evacuation of these 10,000, we told ourselves, would be the last one. The food supply actually increased slightly that month, and a two-week halt of transports in mid-July relieved a lot of anxiety as many concluded the resettlement had ended.

We now know the real cause of that brief lull: Chelmno, in the path of the Red Army, had to be closed and the victims rerouted to a larger and more efficient killing machine—Auschwitz-Birkenau.

On August 2 came the shocking news of deportations on a far greater scale than any of us expected. Placards were posted everywhere, signed by Rumkowski, announcing that, due to impending enemy attack, the whole ghetto had to be evacuated! The destination was unstated but clearly the transfer was to proceed rapidly—5,000 people daily. Entire labor departments, including the workers and their families, machinery and merchandise were slated for removal on successive days in early August. The ghetto was on a schedule to be emptied out within a couple of weeks.

Rumkowski's nearly half-decade-long strategy of "rescue through work" had collapsed. We were no longer useful to the Germans and thus the ghetto had no reason to exist.

Even at this point it never occurred to me, or those close to me, to fight back or escape. Physical resistance was far from the mind of almost every other Jew in the ghetto as well, even those few who, unlike us, knew about the Warsaw ghetto revolt fifteen months earlier. We lacked weapons, of course, as well as connections with anti-fascist Poles. Nearly all of us had been worn down by years of malnutrition and disease. Even if we managed to escape (and to accomplish that we would somehow have to penetrate the formidable fences or walls) what chance would we have as identifiable Polish Jews within the borders of Germany? Our region had neither dense forests, nor friendly peasants, nor roving partisans.

There seemed only two options: wait for our labor departments to be called and report at the Radegast Station as required, or go into hiding in the ghetto and try to hold out until the Soviets arrived. It was not as urgent for Feliks; he could bide his time.

As a policeman he was still assured of steady work and rations and meanwhile might be able to help his family. But Cesia, Vevik, and I and our mothers could receive a knock on the door and a "wedding invitation" any minute. The large Tailor Departments were already being dismantled, all their workers slated for the transports. Our factories could not be far behind.

We three young people stayed up all night grappling with our dilemma. One thing was sure: We had to stay with our mothers. Chana Mest (she had the same first name as my mother) was feeble as well, and neither of the two middle-aged women could survive on her own. Yet, having made the decision for the five of us to stay together, it was still impossible to know if we'd be better off hiding in the ghetto or agreeing to leave.

I certainly understand how people could choose to board those trains. There was no direct evidence that it meant execution and few even mouthed such fears. Looking back at the Holocaust now, we all know the horrific outcome. But while it was happening, most of us could not conceive of annihilation. How could we imagine that people would be forced into gas chambers and asphyxiated? Nothing like that had ever happened in human history.

And there were all sorts of reasons to think you simply were being transferred from one kind of labor camp to another. Weren't they moving equipment as well as workers? Weren't young, skilled, able-bodied people on the transports, as laborers whom the Reich sorely needed? Why would they let us bring our luggage and even allow us to sell our property for cash if they were just going to kill us? And wasn't it plausible that we had to be evacuated because the Lodz ghetto, whose factories were producing so much for the German war effort, was about to be bombed by Allied planes?

Also, word spread that a few dozen people received postcards in late July from loved ones deported the month before. All post-marked on the same day from Leipzig, the brief messages told of families staying together with decent lodging and rations. So maybe the next place wouldn't be so bad.

Beyond all of that, people yearned to leave the ghetto after four and a half years of deprivation and confinement—for me a quarter of my life and my entire youth. None of us had ventured more than a mile or so from our crowded, dilapidated apartments since 1940; we were serving a kind of indeterminate prison sentence. But now it was mid-summer and, strange as it may sound, the idea of going past the barbed wire and traveling into the countryside, even in these wretched circumstances, held a certain appeal. There were young people in the ghetto who could hardly remember what a flower looked like. They longed to gaze out a train window at fertile fields and picturesque villages.

But no matter how we tried to rationalize it, we five couldn't bring ourselves to sit in our apartments, work in our factories, and wait for deportation. Yes, we thought relocation meant hard labor, not a death sentence; yet for our fragile mothers was there really much of a difference? My mother in particular was deteriorating rapidly and I doubted she could withstand even the journey.

Above all, we didn't have an ounce of trust in the authorities. Even though we'd been kept alive for so long, all the promises and propaganda we'd heard from the Germans and Rumkowski now counted for nothing. The worst eventuality had occurred: the ghetto's liquidation had arrived before its liberation.

So we all agreed to go into hiding at once, even before any of us received a notice to report to the train station. By then it might be too late; we had to take action immediately. That would be our form of resistance.

I knew of a place where we could take cover: an attic in a five-story office building in the same courtyard as the headquarters of the meat distribution center. I had needed to come into that compound a few times when I worked at a *Fleischzentralle* outlet back in 1941-42. I can't recall what had brought me up to the attic then; perhaps someone had shown me a potential hideout and it stayed in my mind. Cesia, Vevik and I went there one night to be sure it was unlocked and to check it out. It was only a few blocks from Zydowska Street and all five of us cautiously walked there after nightfall on August 3. I carried my prized winter coat (although I didn't know if I'd live to see another snowfall), a nice dress, and two suits made of material I'd received as a gift when I was engaged at thirteen. Because my growth had been stunted in the ghetto I could still get into those clothes.

Thousands of other Jews were searching for hiding places around the same time—some even burrowing under the walls of the cemetery—but we would have this one to ourselves until the end. Located at Brzezinska Street 40, our refuge actually

The trapdoor leading to the hiding place on 40 Brzezinska as it looks today.

consisted of two roomy attics, the lower one with a couple of windows looking out to the street below; the upper one, accessible by ladder, and with no openings at all. There was not a stick of furniture, so the clothing we brought served as bedding at night, and as seat cushions over the hard wooden floors by day.

Mameh, uprooted from her surroundings, and her body in pain, sat in silence or read her prayer book. Although she'd been a cordial neighbor, she had nothing in common with Chana Mest or her children and had little to say to them now. Still, there was no friction among us and I pushed to the margins of my mind Mameh's strong objections to Vevik. I felt I was with my family, not only my mother but also my husband, sister-in-law, and mother-in-law—if we survived. But I don't recall any of us talking much. We didn't want to make any unnecessary noise, of course, and needed to conserve every bit of strength.

For the first time in many years we were out of sight of the German and Jewish police and freed from the burden of factory labor. But not for a minute did I enjoy the slightest bit of liberty. I felt rather like a hunted animal, knowing the Jewish police were trying to catch us to fill their daily quotas. We could hear the commotion of break-ins and arrests on the neighboring blocks. On the morning of August 9, a nearby house-to-house sweep netted hundreds of fugitives.

But more vividly than anything, I recall the unbearable heat. Because people were in and out of the building during the day, and we were afraid of being detected from the street, we had to stay in the upper attic, which lacked not only windows but also insulation. As the sun beat down, the space became a kind of oven and our mothers suffered terribly. Only late at night did we dare descend to the lower attic, where we felt a slight breeze.

Obviously, nothing was more critical than water and we never had enough. After dark, Cesia, Vevik, or I would quietly venture down to the street, empty our bucket for human waste, and fill another bucket at the nearest communal pump. But often the electricity was off and we had to operate the noisy contraption by hand, a dangerous exercise that could arouse suspicion.

It was even harder getting food. Needless to say we couldn't go to the distribution centers, where we would have been arrested on the spot if we asked for our rations. Most of these outlets were shut anyway, as the ghetto was being closed down. All we could do was come out at night, like rats, and scrounge in garbage bins and vacant lots. But little was to be found beyond some old beet leaves and ersatz coffee grounds. What ghetto dweller threw away anything he could eat? However, we did come across a small wooden barrel of sauerkraut, carried our treasure back to the attic, and tried to make it last.

Spurred by our hunger, we entered private apartments, more and more of which were vacant and unlocked as August ran its course. Once we discovered the corpses of a couple that had starved to death. On the narrow side streets off Brzezinska we stealthily moved northeast toward Marysin, where we knew the Jewish big shots lived, some in villas with gardens. But we never quite made it there; we were afraid to stray too far into unfamiliar territory. If we were caught, we knew our mothers would die in the attic.

Several weeks passed like that, with hunger and thirst far worse even than we'd known as workers. We were all dizzy and listless and looked like walking skeletons. Clearly, our mothers couldn't take more of this punishment—mine had already fainted several times. Then, around August 20, a heat wave arrived with temperatures near 100 degrees. God only knows what a thermometer would have registered in our attic. There was no choice but to leave that furnace and none of us thought differently.

If it had just been Cesia, Vevik and I, we probably would have tried to hold out longer. (Dozens of Jews did just that and came out of hiding when the Red Army finally arrived—almost five months later, on January 19, 1945.) But there was no hope for our mothers in that attic and we wouldn't allow our hiding place to become their death chamber. On the afternoon of August 22, I went outside with the people I loved the most.

Within minutes of stepping on the hot sidewalk we were surrounded by several Jewish policemen, arrested, and marched directly to the train station. For the cops this was quite a haul: five people who didn't have to be rousted out of a building and who didn't put up a struggle. As we walked through the ghetto streets for the last time we saw hundreds of other Jews herded along just like us; evidently the heat and hunger had been a great boon to the predators.

And, as we neared Radegast Station, we joined thousands more Jews, in an outdoor holding pen, out of sight of the rail cars. There weren't enough trains to take us all; we would have to wait.

The delay, of more than twenty-four hours, was awful. We sat on concrete, in the blazing sun. They must have given us a bit of food and water but all I remember is a mass of humanity, worriedly speaking a medley of languages, and beginning to fear the worst.

When our turn finally came it seemed like a relief. The five of us, in a group of about a thousand, were marched hundreds of yards to the transport. I wore my heavy coat in the stifling heat thinking that if it were in my hand it might more easily be taken away from me. And anyway, I needed my arms free to assist my mother.

As soon as I saw the train I realized the hell that was in store. Awaiting us was a line of tall red boxcars with wooden slats, heavy iron doors, and only a small air vent at the top with metal bars across it. These were not passenger coaches but cattle cars!

Shouting SS men prodded us with whips and rifle butts up a narrow wooden plank into the dark compartment. You could hear them counting off the number of people for each car—I think it was a hundred in mine. Yet they had no qualms about closing and locking the door once the exact limit was reached even if it meant breaking up families. Parents were sometimes separated from children *here*, even before the trip to the camps began.

As it turned out, Mameh and I were the last two squeezed into our wagon and Cesia, Vevik, and their mother, just steps behind us, were brutally held back. Their pleas to stay with us were in vain and they were made to board the next car.

An original German Railway cattle car permanently on display today at the Radegast Station in Lodz.

I then heard the doors shut behind me and the metal bolt locked into place.

As soon as my eyes became accustomed to the dim light, and I could see through the crowd, I glimpsed an empty bucket in the middle of the wagon. That would serve as the communal toilet for people of both sexes and all ages. I am told by others who left Lodz in those late August transports that there was a second bucket, of water, and that we were each issued a loaf of bread and a little sugar for the trip. I know it had to be the case, but like the day and night in the holding pen near the station, I recollect no sustenance at all, only hunger and thirst.

There was a lot of agitation around us as people from all walks of life endured this journey of unknown duration to an unknown destination. From the small bit of light that came through the opening above our heads, we could tell we were not traveling west into Germany but rather east into Poland, and that added to the anxiety.

But I thought of nothing except my mother. Not surprisingly, she was in death throes by now. We sat in a corner, and I cradled her head in my lap. "Hold on, Mameh, hold on," I said, as I wiped the perspiration off her brow. Wherever we'd end up, horrible though it might be, perhaps there would be some sort of infirmary that would take her in. With enough water, food, and vitamins she would have at least a chance of survival. "Hold on, Mameh, hold on."

For more than two days we were caged in that cattle car, sometimes moving at a snail's pace, sometimes stopped for hours on a siding. They didn't even open the door to empty the waste bucket; some of the young men spilled its contents through a crack between the floorboards.

We finally arrived not in the middle of the night, as did most transports, but in the morning light. I was temporarily blinded by the sun when the doors swung open but, high off the ground, I could take stock of this place in only a few seconds.

It was pure chaos. Hundreds of exhausted people were being shoved this way and that by wide-eyed men in blue-and-white-striped suits and SS guards with vicious dogs. Chimneys spewed smoke even in the hot sun and a horrible stench filled the air. Watchtowers, barbed wire, and armed sentries were everywhere and in the distance I could make out inmates dressed in rags, their heads completely shaved.

My first thought was that they'd brought us to an insane asylum.

5 The Limit of Human Endurance

I HAD LITTLE TIME TO stare at the scene. The striped-suited men, shouting curses and wielding rubber clubs, entered the cattle car. They ordered my mother and me to leave our few belongings on the train and pushed us down the gangplank into a huge crowd of panicked people.

I soon lost my footing; it was like being tossed around in an angry sea. I held on to Mameh's hand as tightly as I could, while we were prodded and poked from all sides and carried along on a wave of miserable human beings.

Women were being forcibly separated from men and in the distance I spotted Vevik. For a moment our eyes locked. I knew I couldn't make my voice heard over the barking dogs, bellowing guards, and wailing children. Hoping he could read my lips, I mouthed "Be strong." I think I saw him nod before he melted into the mass; I feared it was the last communication we would ever have.

Then my mother was ripped away from me. The guards pulled us apart and pushed us in opposite directions "Hold on, Mameh, we'll meet again," I yelled after her, but I knew she would not be able to survive in this place alone. She was swallowed up by the crush and I was horrified that she'd fall and be trampled to death right there. Later I found out that infirm people like her were put into ambulances marked with Red Cross insignia and driven directly to the gas chambers.

The crowd finally thinned out, the commotion died down, and I found myself in a long line of young women. We were marched along a sandy path up to a dark-haired SS officer with polished boots and a spotless uniform. It was probably the notorious SS doctor Josef Mengele, who made most of the selections at that time. He looked at me for an instant and flicked his wrist. His assistant shouted "*Rechts,*" and I moved to the right.

There were only a few hundred of us by now and we were herded, five abreast, along a lane between two twelve-foot-high wire fences. Signs in German warned that the barriers were electrified and on the steel mesh I saw dead bodies dangling!

Through the fence, many of the inmates stared at us newcomers. The hairless, ragged wretches I'd seen from afar, were now only a few feet away, begging us to throw them any bread we might still be carrying. "They are going to take it away from you, anyway," they claimed. Others—and their guards—moved their fingers across their throats as if to suggest beheading. The men in striped suits keeping us in line were even more direct. They pointed to the chimneys that rose above the camp. "Your families are going up in smoke," they told us with a laugh. My mind could barely absorb those words.

As we entered the large registration building, each of us had to pass in front of a German soldier who confiscated any valuables we had. I saw women forced to surrender jewelry they had managed to keep throughout the entire ghetto period; guards cavalierly tossed watches, rings, necklaces, and bracelets onto a big mound on a table. Some women tried to hide precious objects in their fists or even in their mouths; it was no use. The guards looked under your tongue. With a pair of pliers they pulled out any gold teeth. You also had to give up medicine, photos, letters, prayer books, even eyeglasses—anything on your person.

I had nearly forgotten I was wearing two tiny gold earrings. Shaped like horseshoes, they had been given to me by my father when I was still a baby. I wore them always—they seemed almost a part of my body—and I never thought of selling them in the ghetto despite all the deprivation we faced. Here, of course, I had to hand them over immediately and they, too, were thrown on the pile.

Then we had to go into another room and undress. My winter coat of the past six years, so valuable that I wouldn't risk taking it off in an August heat wave, now fell to the floor. Nor could I keep my prized shoes, for which I had put my life on the line a year earlier. I had to step out of my dress, and my underwear, too. Along with about a dozen other women, I stood naked while a group of male and female German officers, some doctors and some not, inspected us from head to toe. They checked our bellies to make sure that no one who was pregnant had made it through the selection at the railhead. They inspected our private parts to ascertain that no one was hiding anything valuable inside her body.

What did this mean for me, a girl raised in a Chasidic home where modesty was among the highest virtues? Actually, very little. Within the hour, my mother had almost surely been killed. My husband and sister-in-law, who was also my best friend, had been separated from me. Their mother was gone, too. I'd lost the little jewelry and clothing I'd brought along, but worst of all

I'd lost all hope. So what was nakedness and an intrusive body search compared with all that?

The shock was so massive I began to shut down emotionally, to grow numb and follow the curt German commands like I was in a trance.

In the adjoining room a team of women barbers with electric clippers quickly shaved our scalps—and all the rest of our body hair. The prisoners around me became unrecognizable, their heads like strange white globes. Without hair and clothes, they seemed other than female, other than human. I look like that, too, I realized; I look like those freaks I saw when we'd entered the camp.

Next, we were shoved into a delousing chamber and sprayed with a foul-smelling pesticide. Finally, we were issued our camp clothes. Sullen women from behind a counter threw used, dirty garments at us as we walked by; there was not a thought to how they fit. I fared even worse than did the others. I got a thin silk blouse with buttons down the front and a rip in the back. It came down to the upper part of my thighs and barely covered my bottom. For the rest of my time in Auschwitz that was the only piece of clothing I would wear.

As my group was led to our barrack, I began to grasp the magnitude of the camp, designated as Auschwitz II or Birkenau. As far as the eye could see, there were long gray-brown wooden barracks—hundreds of them—arranged in neatly ordered rows. The women's section alone held sixty of these buildings, which housed tens of thousands of females. Even massive Birkenau, I would later learn, was only one part of a giant complex that included the brick headquarter buildings of Auschwitz I, around two miles away, and a half dozen slave labor camps and work sites within a five-mile radius. It was the largest Nazi concentration camp in Europe.

I could already sense that transports like mine were arriving several times a day and that the camp had been pushed far beyond its capacity. Of course, I didn't yet know that nearly half a million Hungarian Jews had been sent to Auschwitz that spring and summer. The arrival of 60,000 Jews from Lodz only accelerated the frenzied killing that prevailed in mid-1944 when Auschwitz became the site of the largest mass murder in human history. While I was there, about ten thousand people were put to death every day.

I entered Block 25, a big shed, something like a stable or cow barn, with a very narrow window across the length of the roof at its peak. Almost a thousand inmates were squeezed into the barrack, obviously intended to accommodate far fewer. Although most people associate Auschwitz with three-tiered bunk beds holding several gaunt prisoners on each level, Block 25 lacked even those primitive berths; we had to sleep on the ground. That meant lying directly on muddy clay soil, dirt that had been

Hungarian Jewish women selected for work at Birkenau on May 1, 1944, less than four months before my arrival. (courtesy USHMM)

On the same day, Hungarian Jewish women after
disinfection and headshaving. (courtesy USHMM)

thrown atop the mass graves of Soviet POWs when the women's camp had been built two years earlier.

Soon the *Blockaelteste*, or head of the barrack, flanked by her underlings, walked out of her little enclosed apartment, the only real living quarters in the structure, and ordered us to stand at attention. Robust and well-fed, she too wore the striped uniform and cap and now I understood that, as in the ghetto, a whole layer of police and functionaries, often Jewish, stood between the Nazi overlords and us slaves. Here a privileged prisoner was called a Kapo, meaning corporal, foreman, or trustee in several European languages. I quickly learned they could be as brutal and sadistic as any German.

The Blockaelteste served as the senior Kapo and ours was a tyrant. Down the middle of the barrack, almost end to end, was a three-foot-high brick divider that looked like a heater, but it was never put in use and served only as a soapbox for her terrifying rants. Atop that platform she strutted back and forth, a thick cane in her right hand. Her opening remarks in Polish that hot August afternoon caused some of the women to collapse in shock.

"I've got news for you," she snarled. "You're all going to die here. Some of you will live two weeks, others four, but you'll all be burned up in the crematorium. In the meantime, you're going to eat and sleep in this barrack, lie in the mud, and obey every rule. If you don't like it, go to the wire!"

Then she retreated to her private rooms. I was stunned like all the others and, like my worst moments in the ghetto, I cried out against the God I'd worshipped as a youngster, the God who now seemed diabolical. But my thoughts quickly turned to a practical matter: I desperately needed a pair of underpants. Whatever time I had left in this world, I couldn't spend it exposed from the waist down. This had nothing to do with modesty: I simply needed some protection from the unimaginable filth of this environment.

So I slipped out of Block 25, not yet realizing how risky it was to walk around without permission. Maybe in another barrack, I told myself with a lot of wishful thinking, they were dispensing more clothing to new arrivals. If not, maybe I could borrow or steal a pair somewhere. I already envisioned the crisp, clean fabric on my skin.

I ducked into Block 24, just across the way, and thought I'd hit the jackpot. It was empty of almost everyone except the Blockaelteste, Golda Katz, who was not only my second cousin, but also someone who owed me a favor! A year and a half earlier, she and her brother Moishe, both more than ten years older than me, had been transferred from their village of Lask to the Lodz ghetto and my family took them in. We shared our cramped quarters with them for many weeks and I gave up my bed, sleeping alongside my mother until they were assigned their own apartment in our building. What phenomenal luck, I thought, to run into Golda, and to have found a protector on my first day in this inferno.

Wearing good shoes, clean clothes, and even a nice sweater, Golda seemed to radiate well being. I ran up to her with open arms and started telling her how I'd been shorted on the clothing line. "Golda! Am I glad to see you! I need ...." She cut me off and told me to get the hell out of her barrack and never come back. Shocked by her glowering eyes, and frightening whip, I didn't dare prolong the discussion but silently turned around and walked away.

I was appalled at this treatment from her, which came on the worst day of my life. The only explanation I have is that Auschwitz often turned ordinary people into heartless animals. (Golda would survive and, after the war, bothered by her conscience, tried to apologize to me with a visit and later a letter, but I could not bear contact with her. *I* shunned *her* when she showed up unannounced, and later tore her letter into tiny pieces without reading it.)

One more time, I tried to obtain a pair of underpants. I entered Block 31, in the next row, and amazingly the Blockaelteste was again someone I knew. Lucja Shymanowska, just a year or two older than me, had lived only a few doors away from my family in pre-war Lodz. Her friendly parents were frequent customers of our grocery store and our mothers often talked together in the afternoons.

Yet now I beheld a ferocious beast. I stood at the rear of the barrack just as she was delivering the "introductory lecture" to her prisoners: "You whores! You bitches!" she shouted. "You think you came to a resort? Well, I built this place and it's no resort. You'll never leave here alive."

Suddenly her eye caught someone in the front row, whom I

also recognized from Lodz. Lucja stopped speaking and began slugging that woman with a club. I winced as I saw the heavy blows rain down on her head. Blood spurted from her face. Then she fell to the floor and stopped moving. A Kapo dragged her body out the door, and I realized that I'd just witnessed a killing. I feared I could be next. Very cautiously I exited block 31, hoping Lucja hadn't noticed me. My reconnaissance trip to the neighboring barracks and my quest for underwear was over.

Like a beaten dog, I returned to Block 25. I would remain there for the next six weeks, starved, terrorized, and lying half-naked in muck.

Those who have read about Auschwitz-Birkenau, perhaps in the writings of Elie Wiesel or Primo Levi, learn of a camp society. A pecking order developed based on how long one had been interned; the veterans even received a grudging respect from the Kapos. With a brisk black market, it was possible to obtain items like spoons, combs, soap, toothbrushes, and cigarettes. A few inmates, usually non-Jews, even received packages or letters from the outside. Male captives occasionally entered the women's camp as repairmen allowing for some contact between the sexes. Most prisoners left Birkenau during the day in work crews and sometimes obtained food or information from local peasants. At night in the barracks one could hear songs, stories, and even prayers.

But that was not my experience. Block 25, although situated amidst the others, was in a special category—a holding pen for the doomed. The over-capacity of the killing machine spared us from the gas chambers *for the time being*, but the women in our barrack, nearly all Polish Jews, were deemed unfit for work and slated for extermination. I received no identifying triangle to wear on my clothes, no tattoo on my arm. I was thrown in there like a piece of garbage before it was to be incinerated.

Why Block 25 was my fate I'll never know. Young and relatively healthy, I should have been assigned to a regular barrack. But I arrived at the peak of crowding and chaos; perhaps they intended to dispose of everyone in my transport, the strong along with the weak, but needed some of us to wait our turn. Perhaps it was just a bureaucratic mistake. Whatever the reason, it put me into the innermost circle of hell short of the gas chambers.

Aside from the lack of bunks, we were denied other pitiful "amenities" afforded most of the inmates. They received a "breakfast" of watery ersatz coffee and a piece of bread while our only meal was a mid-day soup and sometimes we failed to get even that. If other prisoners became sick, there was at least the possibility of being sent to the prison infirmary; none of us ever got even that slim chance at recovery. Other inmates usually wore wooden clogs while we went barefoot. Once, when I found a pair of clogs in a corner of the barrack and put them on, I was given a beating for breaking the rules.

Conditions in Block 25 were so horrific that I felt under torture every day I was there. The thirst during the day could drive one insane; the hunger in the evening eclipsed everything else. So many women were jammed into our barrack that it was impossible to sleep without literally being under or on top of someone, and quarrels and scuffles constantly erupted. Cries like, "Your foot is in my mouth" or "Your elbow hit me in the eye" were heard throughout the night. Not that anyone could truly rest anyway. The atrocities one witnessed during the day invaded one's dreams at night.

As in the ghetto, lice and rodents were rampant and in such tight quarters, and with such malnutrition and slime, infectious diseases were the rule. Typhoid, dysentery, and pneumonia were so widespread in our barrack that for several weeks we were under quarantine. The Kapos still ran the place but the SS was afraid to enter in order to make its selections. At least this stayed our execution.

While we sat and waited for death I saw women with the most gruesome rashes and sores from their illnesses, as well as broken bones and infected wounds from having been beaten. The undernourishment caused our breasts to sag and almost vanish on our chests. We all seemed about half our normal body weight.

Although we were never sent out for hard labor, a backbreaking task was required of us nonetheless. It was roll call, or *Apell* in German, occurring twice a day whether we were under quarantine or not. Well before dawn we were awakened, marched outside our barrack, and forced for three or four hours to stand *or kneel*, motionless and not even permitted to cough. When the sun finally rose, it beat down mercilessly on our bald heads.

The Kapos counted us again, and again, and again. The number changed daily because some prisoners had died overnight or been selected for the gas chambers the day before, and others came into our block. Nearly all of Birkenau's 200,000 inmates endured the roll call at the same time, and if a person in any barrack was missing, the grueling wait usually continued for all of us until he or she was accounted for.

In the late afternoon, a second Apell was called, another ordeal that could last for hours. When it rained, or got colder, there was no change in the routine and I nearly froze in my skimpy blouse. My muscles ached terribly but I knew that to collapse would result in a whipping if not worse.

After the morning Apell, the Blockaelteste usually gave the command for us to use the latrines—the only time, day or night, that we were permitted to do so. The "toilets," out in the open, consisted of about a hundred holes in wooden planking over a ditch. The openings were so close together that your body often touched the person next to you. Many hundreds of women had to use these latrines; the "bathroom break" for our entire barrack was limited to fifteen minutes, so there was a lot of jostling and shoving to get to those holes. During your turn—God forbid if you took a little extra time—a stronger woman might push you off. A few yards away there was a trough with several faucets, from which murky water flowed, but these taps were always mobbed and one had to be very aggressive and lucky to get to the head of the line. Needless to say, there were no towels or toilet paper. Human waste was everywhere, even on the wooden boards we had to sit on, and the stench from that area was indescribable.

Obviously, we needed to relieve ourselves at other times but were strictly required to hold it in. Among my strongest memories of Auschwitz is the near-constant urgency I felt to urinate. I know that other barracks had a bucket for inmates to use during the night, which was taken out and emptied when it became full. This was not the case in Block 25.

Naturally, accidents occurred frequently and, again, the punishment was a sound thrashing. I was once severely beaten for this myself, and the Kapo called me a pig while she administered the blows. Like many of the women I suffered from diarrhea and couldn't control my bowels regardless of the penalty. Yet if your neighbor did not report you, the stink did not always give you away because it was barely more pungent than the horrid smell of nearly a thousand sick, sweaty females, many of them dying, and none of whom was ever allowed a bath or shower.

We did not have to worry, however, about menstruation; I never heard of anyone who had her period in Birkenau. There was a rumor that the Germans put *Brum*, or bromide into our soup to prevent the monthly blood flow, but more likely the hunger and stress in the camp was responsible for our failure to menstruate. Women in other parts of Auschwitz were sometimes worried that they might never get their periods again and so might never be able to have children. I doubt that anyone in Block 25 thought so far into the future.

In those first days, I considered suicide many times. I deeply regretted not having taken poison back in the ghetto, which would have spared me the agony of the cattle train and now the death factory. It is impossible for any human being to endure this, I quickly concluded. Envying the dead, I was sorely tempted to throw myself on the 5,000-volt fence and with one jolt end it all. Women ran to the wire almost every day in a bid to exercise control over their deaths even as they had lost all control over their lives. In that sense I sometimes viewed suicide as a brave act and one that I didn't carry out simply because I lacked the courage.

But as time passed I began to feel differently. My numbness and self-pity turned to hatred and anger toward my jailers. The first stirrings of my will to live in Auschwitz were born out of a desire to get back at them.

How could such killers be allowed to go unpunished? Not only did they delight in every bit of anguish we felt, but also they had coolly calculated how to break us down. Nothing here, beginning with the shaved heads and ending with the chimney smoke, was an accident. The salty soup that heightened our thirst, the lavatory rules that stole the last shred of human dignity, the monotonous roll calls that caused such pain all were part of a demonic plan to torment us even while we awaited extermination. Sometimes, during the endless Apell, I could glimpse the water trough and see the faucets, so near and yet so far. They were purposely left dripping, I was sure, as part of the overall scheme to drive us mad.

I dreamed of taking revenge once the tables were turned. All I had left now was my imagination and incredible scenarios of reprisal took hold of my mind: how I'd cut open their flesh and rub salt in the wounds, how I'd tie their limbs to horses that would be sent running in different directions. The Blockaelteste, the SS men, the Kapos would all suffer just as I had been made to suffer.

I thought, too, of my four loved ones who had hidden with me in that sweltering attic in the ghetto and were now in Auschwitz. The gray smoke and orange flames coming out of the towering chimneys answered any question I had about my mother and Chana Mest; I saw no Jew their age among the living. Cesia could be languishing in a nearby barrack, I figured, and my new husband might be only a few hundred yards from me, fighting for his life in the men's camp on the other side of an electrified fence.

Yet I didn't let myself be consumed by the great loss I'd sustained or by worry for others. If I was going to try to survive, my instincts told me, I couldn't allow my strength to be sapped either by grief for the dead or anxiety for the living. It was as if my prior relationships belonged to another world. Besides, I was in such physical agony that it was hard to think about anything but my empty stomach, parched mouth, or aching bones—and the revenge to be taken later.

But I did not feel alone in Auschwitz. From the beginning I formed a close bond with four other Jewish girls from my transport, about my age. I knew two of them from Lodz; they were from religious families and my father and theirs had studied Talmud together.

The authorities required units of five for everything—roll call, marching to the latrines, lining up for inspections—and we were arbitrarily assigned to comprise such a unit. Unlike most other fivesomes, however, we vowed at the outset to help one another survive. We didn't know the English phrase "All for one, and one for all" but that described us perfectly. I now had a new family to replace the one I'd just lost.

We volunteered as a group to bring the vats of soup from the kitchen to the barrack, a distance of about fifty yards. Few prisoners wanted to perform this work. The hot soup was dispensed in bulky steel cauldrons, each weighing almost a hundred pounds and requiring two people as carriers. Most women could barely lift that much and had to stop many times along the way. Beyond the hard labor, on slippery, muddy walkways, the task also meant more contact with the Kapos, both in the kitchen and the barracks, and thus the risk of arbitrary beatings.

I wanted to take the chance, however, and my friends agreed. Because of my prior work in the soup kitchen and later the meat distribution center in the Lodz ghetto, I knew the advantages of working around food.

None of us five actually doled out the soup, which might contain some barley or turnips but also insects and mice. That right was reserved for the Blockaelteste and the Kapos. Since it was the only nourishment we ever received, whether it was a watery serving from the top of the vat or a thick one from the bottom, the soup could sometimes be the difference between life and death. My four Auschwitz sisters and I often received skimpy portions ourselves, ladled into a small tin cup, the insides of which we lapped like dogs, yet another humiliation.

But as I'd hoped, we five had an opportunity to snatch some of the precious liquid on the long walk back from the kitchen to the barrack. At first we just took turns scooping it up in our hands, but then we found a better way. One of my comrades discovered a good-sized empty can somewhere and hid it in the folds of the skirt she'd been issued. With fibers torn from our clothing we fashioned a set of strings, sturdy enough to tie the can to the inner part of one of the girl's thighs. Just accomplishing that task raised our morale.

Once we were out of sight of the kitchen guards, the girl would take out the can and we'd fill it with soup. We passed it around as we lugged the big barrels, each of us quickly downing a few gulps. Then the can went back to its holder and we'd enter Block 25 trying to look as famished as everyone else. That our robbery effectively deprived some other women in the barrack of a bit of soup didn't even cross my mind. Conventional moral concerns applied here even less than they did in the ghetto.

Stealing the soup required a lot of teamwork and mutual trust. A mistake by one of us could have had the most severe consequences for all five. But we learned the drill well and performed it every day in under a minute. We were never caught and I'm convinced that my survival depended not only upon the food I filched, but also on the companionship I felt.

As close as I was to the other four girls, we spoke little of our lives before the war or about our hopes for the future. We did talk about survival strategies: how to raise the odds against being selected for extermination (pinch your cheeks as hard as you can), how to guard against dysentery (don't drink from the puddles of water on the ground), how to keep out of the way of the Kapos (refrain from making eye contact). We five also shared our wild fantasies of revenge against our oppressors.

Today, I can't recall the girls' names or remember their faces. If the people I loved before Auschwitz were no longer my main concern once I entered that universe, neither would the friendships I formed there continue once I left.

Each of us five also kept a lot inside. That became horribly clear one night when one of the group, a formerly attractive girl from a good family, ran to the wire and was electrocuted. She bolted from the barrack one night while we slept, and we saw her hanging on the wire during the morning Apell. None of the other four of us had an inkling that she was contemplating suicide; had we suspected it, we would have done everything in our power to prevent it. Another young woman quickly took her place in our unit.

Who could blame someone for taking her own life? The physical torment and mental anguish never ceased. Except for the quarantine period, every week or so SS men came into our barrack and selected many of us for the gas chambers. All it took was an injury, an illness, or just bad luck. You couldn't put this out of your mind for one moment because the fetid odor of burning flesh permeated everything. While I was in Auschwitz, bodies were burned not only in the crematoria, but also in open pits. Death was literally in the air.

The stench was such, I thought at the time, that it should have been smelled all over the world and the screams heard in the heavens. In fact, Auschwitz was well observed from above. American Air Force reconnaissance planes photographed the whole complex in the summer of 1944. In those pictures, which now hang in Yad Vashem and the U.S. Holocaust Memorial Museum, clearly visible are the barracks, crematoria, and tall chimneys of the camp. But the Allies, who bombed oil refineries and munitions plants nearby, did nothing to slow the killing machine.

Yet deliverance of a sort arrived in early October, and had it not, I soon would have died of the cold, now a greater threat than hunger, disease, or even the gas chamber. At times, we were actually allowed to sit or lie outside the barrack and warm ourselves in the early afternoon sun. But soon it got quite chilly both inside the unheated block and out, and the miserable garment I wore offered scant protection. Only because we slept close together— the five of us were inseparable nights as well as days—could we feel any warmth at all. I could not contemplate surviving the late fall, much less the winter, in Birkenau; a dip in the temperature of merely a few more degrees surely would have killed me.

Luckily, the German high command found use for some of the inmates of Block 25. With its military position rapidly eroding in the early autumn of 1944—the Reich was being heavily bombed and German borders had been crossed by American soldiers in the west and the Red Army in the east—the Wehrmacht needed every possible pair of hands for the war effort. One cold day our entire barrack was lined up for the last selection: Each of us would be chosen either for work in a slave labor camp in Germany, or for asphyxiation. The chief camp doctor, Josef Mengele, decided who would live and who would die.

Like the many past selections, when mid-level SS officers entered our barrack and in a matter of seconds determined the fate of each woman, we lied to one another and to ourselves about our chances. Even someone who could barely stand hoped to pass the ultimate test.

Roughly five hundred women were lined up and well over half of us were condemned to die, but my entire unit of five was among the exactly two hundred spared. We were informed that we'd be leaving camp that evening (which was October 3 according to camp records I examined many years later). Although dazed by a month-and-a-half ordeal and shivering, I was overjoyed at the news. I would walk out of Auschwitz after all, and it was inconceivable that the next place could be as bad.

But my life nearly ended on the way to the railway station, a harrowing trek of many miles, from early morning to late at night in freezing rain. Barefoot and still wearing nothing but that flimsy blouse, it felt like I was walking on ice. I didn't think I could make it. After a few hours, I was so cold and so weak that my legs could no longer carry me. I could feel my heart slowing.

I knew that to collapse, or just stop and rest, meant a bullet to the back of the neck. But despite that and everything I'd already been through, the pain was too excruciating for me to go on. "I can't take it any more. I give up," I told the other four girls in my group, and I dropped to the ground.

"We won't let you die here," my fellow soup-carriers retorted. They picked me up, slapped my face, and got me moving again. I had been at the end of the row, where the wind and rain were fiercest, so first they moved me to the middle spot and then the girls on either side of me warmed my body with theirs. They reached under my arms and carried me for a stretch, taking the pressure off my weary legs. I lost consciousness for a while but somehow I made it to the station.

We were processed in the terminal—in a heated hall. At first, the spike in temperature was a shock to our systems and many of us were overcome with stomach cramps and diarrhea. There was a mad, animal-like rush for a single waste pail and for a while I wondered how far from Auschwitz I'd really come.

But soon I began to feel a lot better. We were issued wooden clogs and adequate if oversized, clothing, including big overcoats. I had enough extra fabric on the dress I was given that I could tear some of it off to make a belt and kerchief. And then we got something I could have only dreamed about—a hot shower. That evening we were allowed to rest on cots with blankets.

We regained some of our strength at the way station and a few nights later we were on the move again. Just before we boarded the train, some Polish women in blue uniforms with white caps and aprons—they might have been nuns or Red Cross nurses—served us tea from large kettles. I've wondered ever since if they had any idea how much that act of human kindness meant.

6 From Slavery to Freedom

THE CROWDED CATTLE CAR, WITH a single bucket for human waste, was similar to the transport that had brought us from the ghetto to Auschwitz. Again our destination was unknown. Yet now the mood was different. Back in the August heat, chaos had reigned as the elderly, the sick, and the children screamed for food or water. But this train, carrying the small remnant to have come out alive, was somber and subdued. With grim determination, we prepared ourselves for the next trial.

Through the night the railcars rolled west, deep into Germany. In the darkness, I had lost track of my four Auschwitz sisters and began talking quietly with someone else, a bright young woman, a few years older than me. Regina Jakobowitz and I had a lot in common and we bonded immediately. It turned out that we had lived on the same street in the ghetto. I had no memory of her but we knew many of the same people. The Jakobowitz family resided in Baluty before the war like my husband and sister-in-law, Vevik and Cesia Mest. Regina's younger brother, Fred, frequented the Mests' family-run barbershop and I had met the likeable Fred a few times after my family moved to the ghetto.

Regina's parents, like mine, had operated a successful business before the war and, although hers were not Chasidic, they were quite observant. But she and her two brothers also embraced popular Polish music, literature, and movies. The entire Jakobowitz family was deported to Auschwitz in the same cattle car. The father died en route and Regina, like me, was separated from her frail mother on the day they arrived, never to see her again. Her brothers were sent to the men's camp and now their whereabouts were unknown. Regina was assigned to Block 31, into which I had stumbled on my first day in Birkenau and where I witnessed the terror inflicted by her notorious *Blockaelteste,* Lucja Shymanowska.

Two other girls in the car, the lively sisters Manya and Franya, joined us to form a little clique. They had grown up near me in Gorny Rynek and I remembered them well. Their mother shopped in our store and their father studied in Tateh's circle. Even before our journey ended, we four somehow knew we'd remain together. I was now part of yet another spontaneous group that functioned almost like a family. The brief, yet intense attachments that sprung up during the war comforted me no end.

But where were we headed? In the morning light, one girl peered through the narrow opening at the top of the car and recognized the Elbe River and the domes of great Baroque churches and palaces. "That's Dresden," she said, identifying the legendary seat of the Saxon kings and one of the most beautiful and cultured cities in Germany. In less than an hour the train came to a halt and the doors swung open.

We had stopped at a camp about thirty miles southwest of

Dresden in the outskirts of a small town called Oederan. The exact date, I learned much later, was October 9, 1944. We were marched through an opening in the barbed wire fence by the Germans who had guarded us on the train—this late in the war they were boyish teens or older men. We underwent no selections and saw no crematoria. It seemed that our masters wanted to keep us alive, at least while we could be useful to them.

Because of the Reich's wartime needs and the unlimited greed of its corporations, millions of prisoners who could still work—Jews and non-Jews—were exploited as slave laborers, many in the highly industrialized state of Saxony. Even in the fall of 1944, the deluded German leaders were still in a mad rush to produce every weapon they could. They refused to acknowledge that the war was already lost.

Our sub-camp was one of almost a hundred in the vast Flossenberg complex that stretched across this region and beyond. But Oederan itself, housing five hundred women, seemed compact to me—one large, square wooden barrack, divided into three halls, alongside a factory, which was busy day and night.

Living conditions bore little resemblance to Auschwitz. I was given my own berth on the bottom of a two-tiered bunk and slept on a thin mattress filled with straw, under a blanket made of synthetic material. The barrack was heated, if poorly. We received a hot drink and a piece of bread in the morning before work, and soup and more bread in the evening. The greatest luxury of all was a hot communal shower in the basement of the barrack once a week, for which we were each issued a bar of "soap." It was not the real thing but a substance made largely of sand. We had neither toothbrushes nor toothpaste, so I brushed my teeth using some of that gritty ersatz soap on my finger. One woman "pressed" a pair of pants by placing it between two boards and sleeping on top. Indeed, most of us were quite resourceful when it came to health and grooming.

Although I was known only by a number sewn on the dress I'd been issued at the way station after Auschwitz, in Oederan I actually began to feel a bit of femininity again. My hair was staring to grow back and no one required that our scalps be shaved. You could go to the outhouse simply by asking permission, which was usually granted, though of course you didn't dare linger.

In Birkenau's Block 25, every day had been the same but here we toiled during the week and were granted one day off, Sunday, when we were free to move around the entire barrack and socialize with the other inmates. We sought to entertain one another with stories, songs, and even interpretive dance.

We also tried to teach one another skills and put an ounce of creativity into our lives. I improved my sewing ability and with a couple of other girls tried to fashion a bra from a discarded piece of fabric. What did I use for a needle and thread? A rigid piece of straw and a fiber pulled from my oversized dress.

But I don't want to paint too rosy a picture of Oederan, which had its share of brutality and misery. Prisoners were beaten to death on occasion and others died from the harsh conditions. I never got seriously ill myself, but many women suffered from dysentery, tuberculosis, and pneumonia. The infirmary was always crowded and few actually came back from there.

Not the least of our problems was the friction among the various ethnic groups. We were nearly all Jews, but only about half of us were Polish. The rest were mostly Czech and Hungarian. Every section in the sprawling barrack had women from all three countries; I think the Nazis purposely mixed us together to minimize camaraderie and sow discord.

Basic communication was possible because nearly all of us understood some Yiddish. But while the Czechs and Poles usually got along—I even learned the Czech language, which bears some similarity to Polish—the Hungarians, mostly religious women from small *shtetls*, stuck to their own kind. After Auschwitz, Jewish ritual held little meaning for me, so I was surprised to see them still *daven*. Their praying was none of my business, of course, but I was offended by how they looked down on the rest of us as goyim because we weren't observant. I didn't believe in God anymore but I had never felt more Jewish. Was there any other reason all this was happening to us?

During Passover, many of the Hungarians made a big show out of not eating bread. We were all famished yet they vowed to deny themselves both the morning and evening slices of the forbidden food and subsist only on soup. But when the bread came around, they didn't refuse it. Instead, they hoarded it, thinking that when the eight days were over they'd gorge themselves. Sure enough, the mounting piles of bread invited theft. Accusations flew and then fistfights erupted among the Magyar women and between them and the Czechs and Poles. It was a cruel mockery of Passover. Regina later told me of a female Hungarian Kapo in Auschwitz who savagely beat prisoners during the day and fervently recited prayers at night. In the camps, as in normal life, religious practice and human decency did not always go hand in hand.

Although some of the inmates had privileged positions, there were no Kapos in Oederan. Rather, the barrack was directly controlled by about a dozen SS females, trained at the notorious women's concentration camp at Ravensbrueck. Most of them had served in Auschwitz or other death camps and been hardened into violent taskmasters. My Blockaelteste, a young, attractive blonde, was relatively humane although it was not uncommon for her to beat us with a hard rubber club. She showed no leniency if you were late to the morning or evening *Apell*, the bone-chilling roll calls that were only a little shorter than those in Birkenau. While there were few suicides in Oederan, the unbearable pressure of camp life caused some of the women to descend into madness. At night we were sometimes woken up by the shrieks of those who had gone insane.

Worst of all was the drudgery of a twelve-hour shift in the poorly heated plant, a former dyeing factory, recently converted to a munitions factory by a company called Deutsche Kuehl-und-Kraftmaschinen or DKK. It had produced industrial refrigerators and now sought to enrich itself in the arms industry. Ironically, it still exists in Germany with a progressive reputation as the producer of appliances that don't harm the environment.

Beginning with our arrival, DKK turned out explosive rounds for aircraft cannon, and our job was to manufacture the payload. Along with about two hundred women, I did the same thing all day, six days a week: drill a hole several inches into the hard metal nose of the rounded, oblong-shaped rockets. We stacked these in crates, which were taken to another factory nearby, where male slave laborers filled the holes with explosive powder.

It was the most arduous work I've ever performed in my life, much harder than the labor in the ghetto. For all of the vaunted German technology, the four-foot-high machine, with its clanking metal chains, was not powered by an electric motor. For more than half a year in Oederan, I had to use both hands to turn the crank of that contraption inflicting serious injury to my neck, shoulders, and back. I am still in pain from it today.

Time moved very slowly on the factory floor and at the beginning of each shift it seemed like an eternity lay before me. They permitted only a fifteen-minute break every few hours and my undernourished body, further punished by the cold, rebelled every time I rotated the handle. Thankfully, I was never assigned the even more harrowing night shift.

Naturally, the thought of sabotage crossed my mind. After all,

I was producing weapons for the very regime that had murdered my family and was intent on killing me eventually. What if I drilled the holes too short or too long, or at the wrong angle? What if I broke the bit or disabled the machine? I was so embittered at that point I might well have tried to undermine the system had it meant putting only my own life at risk. But I knew if I were found out, there would be reprisals against my campmates as well. I could envision the SS hanging ten women for such an act. So I just continued to do what they told me. Merely slowing down the pace would have been asking for big trouble—for all of us.

At night I'd return to the barrack aching, freezing, and hungry. But then at least I was with my friends.

Regina worked on a similar machine a few rows away from me and suffered in the same way; we tried to lift one another's spirits in the evening and were often joined by Manya and Franya. Manya was extremely lucky: She was not assigned to the plant but rather to the kitchen where there were many opportunities to swipe some extra food and dispose of the evidence by swallowing it right there. All four of us benefited when she was able to snatch a pile of potato peels, boil them, and smuggle the treasure into the barrack. She'd wait until late at night when everyone was asleep and then wake us up to share in this bounty. We were giddy with excitement during those midnight snacks.

There was another way I staved off hunger that meant a lot more. Soon after my arrival in Oederan, I was astonished when one of the German civilian foremen, a tall guy in his sixties with salt and pepper hair, came over to my machine to oil it, and dropped something wrapped in paper into the bucket for the metal shavings below. Bending over, he whispered in my ear in German that his wife had sent it and added, "Hold on, it won't take long until the war is over."

After he moved to the next workstation, I peeked inside the

wrapper and beheld a salami sandwich! It would be too dangerous to eat it in the factory, so I hid it under my bulky clothing and
shared it with Regina that night.

My angel repeated his good deed *several times a week* during
almost my entire imprisonment there. When not salami, it was
liverwurst, ham, or cheese—precisely the protein and fat which
our diet lacked and that we craved. At this stage in the war, food
was rationed for German civilians, so he and his family could not
have had a lot to spare. But whether or not his good deed resulted
in hardship, there is no question it put him in danger. There was
a strict prohibition against fraternizing with inmates; in order to
provide me that nourishment he put his life on the line. For about
two weeks he was away from his job and I dreaded that he'd been
found out and severely punished. But he was missing for some
other reason; he returned and resumed his courageous caring.

Who was this German hero? What motivated him? Did he
sustain other girls or just me? I never found out the answers and
one of my deepest regrets is that I didn't return to Oederan after
the war to look him up and thank him. Even though I didn't have
his name or address, and Oederan ended up in the Soviet zone of
occupation, I might have been able to find him. I learned much
later that another kindly foreman in the camp, also too old to be
at the front, gave out sweets along with copies of the New Testa-
ment. But my righteous gentile, my *Schindler*, neither spread the
Gospel nor asked for anything in return, while he nurtured me
with hope along with food.

Others helped too but their motives were not as pure. For a
while, our good-looking SS Blockaelteste took a liking to me and
I became her pet. First, she arranged an enormous change for
the better in my daily schedule. Instead of slaving in the noisy
factory, I spent all day seated in a quiet, pleasant room—knitting
a sweater for this woman who had the power of life and death

over me. My muscles soon relaxed and the pain eased. And I didn't even have to forgo the sandwiches dropped in the shavings. I don't recall how, but the foreman knew to leave them with Regina while I was away.

Meanwhile, my SS protector started sweet-talking me with fond phrases. *Du bist ein huebsches Maedchen,* she'd say affectionately, "You are a pretty girl." It didn't occur to me that this might have sexual overtones. I was so naïve that I barely knew of the existence of male homosexuality, and had no inkling at all about lesbianism.

Besides, I couldn't imagine that anyone would be physically attracted to me in Oederan, and not only because I was a scrawny, scruffy slave laborer. In Auschwitz, I had developed a growth on my lip at the corner of my mouth. Now it was getting worse. As large as the digit of a finger, it was turning blue and looked awful. Even in this environment, it made me feel self-conscious.

"I'll bring you to the infirmary and we'll have it removed," suggested my all-powerful new friend. But the prospect of a Nazi doctor taking a scalpel to my face was horrifying—this was no place for elective surgery. I refused her offer, which took all the bravery I could summon, for I knew how easily one day's favorite could become the next day's outcast.

As I feared, after less than a week in the paradise of the sewing room, I was ordered back to bondage on the factory floor. I had not only gone against the Blockaelteste's wishes, but I remained with a big imperfection and could not become the object of her desire if that is what she hoped. I learned much later that homosexual abuse was rampant in many slave labor camps and also occurred in ours, so I'll never know if the growth on my face spared me from something worse.

A few days after my fall from grace, I was straggling back from the evening Apell, perhaps a moment late. Suddenly, I felt a hard blow to the back of my head. I turned around and saw the blonde Blockaelteste. She beat me repeatedly until I collapsed.

We all felt that 1945 would be the last year of the war. In addition to the uplifting words of the German foreman, rumors came to us from a nearby British POW camp, some of whose inmates had been on the battlefield in the past year. I never saw those prisoners myself but a few of the women in my camp encountered them on work details and picked up a bit of news. The information was sketchy, but we didn't doubt that Hitler's armies were in full retreat. Months earlier, in the final days of the Lodz ghetto, I had been bitterly disappointed waiting for the Red Army, but now my hopes rose again.

The best war news came in the form of the nighttime Allied bombings to which we were exposed because the many arms factories in our area were high-value targets. There was never a direct hit on Oederan but we sometimes heard the hum of British and American aircraft followed by sirens and then explosions. Our German guards ran to air raid shelters, while we were locked in the barrack and ordered to remain in our bunks. Instead, we ran to the windows and looked out for signs of damage.

I felt more elation than fear. Sure, I could be injured or killed, but that was a risk I gladly took, knowing the plant might be wrecked and the SS could become casualties too. It was worth a lot to me just to see the panic in their eyes as they scurried away. You could tell that even beyond their immediate physical safety, they dreaded the coming end of the Reich. What would be their fate, they worried, if captured by the Soviets?

Bombing runs continued throughout the winter but nothing prepared us for the night of February 13, 1945. It sounded like every plane in the Allied air force was aloft and we braced ourselves for something terrific. First came boom after boom in the distance, the reverberations shaking the floor. Then, in the direction of Dresden, we saw several red-orange blazes leaping high against the black sky. Soon they converged to form one soaring fireball turning night into day. For hours the blasts continued and the colossal conflagration grew to Biblical proportions.

We were ecstatic. Hugging and kissing one another, we sang and danced and cried with joy. Every building in Dresden must be burning, we jubilantly convinced ourselves—the renowned city had to be a charred ruin. This is it, we all agreed, the payback we'd been waiting for and the finale of our long oppression. Further raids were carried out the next morning and we cheered those as well. If the black soot in the air made it difficult for us to breathe, that was all the better. We tried to hide our emotions when the downcast German guards reappeared—you could get whipped for just a smirk—but I'm sure they knew what we were feeling.

In fact, I had witnessed something even greater than I'd realized at the time, one of the most destructive nights in all of European history. Because the center of Dresden, rich in cultural landmarks, was of no military or strategic significance, many Germans thought it would never be bombed and sought refuge there, doubling up with family or friends. It was a terrible miscalculation. Almost a thousand British planes, sent as retaliation for the Luftwaffe's bombing of London and Coventry and also to avenge much else, dropped a record amount of explosives on the Saxon capital. It resulted in a raging firestorm with winds so strong that objects and people were literally sucked into its 600-degree core. Several square miles of historical Dresden were obliterated.

That firebombing has remained one of the great moral controversies of World War II. Was it right for Churchill to have ordered an attack that killed so many civilians—25,000 is the current consensus, although far higher body counts have been given—

and laid waste to so many masterpieces of art and architecture? Several leading German thinkers have pointed to Dresden as an example of an Allied atrocity and tried to equate it with Nazi barbarity. Even some Jewish concentration camp prisoners who rejoiced in the firestorm at the time, later expressed remorse for the pleasure they felt that night.

I have no patience with this sort of hand wringing. The devastation of Dresden came to us as a gift from the heavens, a sign that there was at least a bit of fairness in the universe. It occurred only because a criminal regime had murdered tens of millions of innocent men, women, and children. Nazism enjoyed nearly the full support of the German people and I got some satisfaction when at long last the fire scorched some of them too. But most of all, I was thrilled because I was sure the war would now be over. Even the madmen in Berlin, I thought, would have to surrender in the face of the awesome power I'd just witnessed.

Sadly, though, the firestorm did not bring an immediate end to the hostilities in Europe as the atom bomb later did in the Pacific. Nor did it end our suffering. Oederan continued to function at high capacity for another two months and my friends and I remained enslaved until the day it closed. Even then we would not be liberated. Far from it.

Not until April 14, 1945, with the Soviets halfway across Saxony, did the SS abandon Oederan. Still, they would not abandon *us*, we who could attest to their murderous deeds. They probably thought of exterminating all the survivors then and there but lacked the time and equipment. Instead, they decided to ship us off to a concentration camp with adequate killing facilities.

We went on a military freight train, accompanied by most of Oederan's women SS but we saw little of them on the journey. They traveled in their own heated, closed carriage, but forced us into open coal cars, each carrying about seventy prisoners with barely enough room to sit down. A layer of black dust was still on the surface of the bare steel wagon-bed and walls. I had thought that the cattle car was the cruelest means of transportation. I was wrong.

The SS must have expected to deliver a lot of dead bodies because we were provided nothing to eat or drink during a voyage that lasted a full week. Indeed, many of the women died en route, their corpses decomposing as we traveled. The living lay intermixed among the dead.

What saved some of us, including Regina, Manya, Franya, and me, was the pity of some German farmers we passed along the way. They seemed both curious and embarrassed that human beings, females no less, could have fallen so low, and that other people, their own countrymen, had caused this to happen. Many of the bystanders averted their eyes and walked away. But a few whom we begged for food did try to relieve our hunger; they threw us beets, potatoes, and cow fodder from their trucks or carts. Needless to say, we fought like beasts over these offerings, which were still caked in soil. For some of the farmers, our wretched appearance and wild behavior must have confirmed their belief that Jews were savages.

Only infrequently would a civilian bring us a bucket of water, and dehydration posed as great a threat as did hunger. But it rained a lot that April, so we cupped our hands and drank whatever fell from the sky. The storm clouds had another advantage: they kept the Allied bombing runs to a minimum. Looking from the air like a German troop train, we could easily have been strafed and we lacked even a roof over our heads.

When would this horror come to an end? Back and forth went our train, east and then west, north and then south. I later learned that Buchenwald, a likely endpoint, was less than a hundred miles from Oederan but it had been liberated by the Americans on April 11. A couple of days earlier, 1,200 Jewish inmates there had been locked into freight cars by the SS and abandoned on a remote siding. GIs discovered them two weeks later, all dead. We were close to a similar fate.

Our railcars, though, were not sealed and since we were not guarded closely, we could have jumped off and tried to run away. Even in a German village someone might have sheltered a few of us in an attic or barn, perhaps reasoning that harboring victims of fascism might look good in the eyes of the Red Army, which could arrive at any time. But escape quickly became impossible. Within a couple of days on that train, nearly all of us were sapped of strength and close to delirium. The hunger was like nothing I'd known even in Block 25. For sixty-six months, benefiting from the help of friends and strangers, I had clawed my way to survival hour by painful hour. Yet now, as the energy drained out of my body, it all seemed in vain. In that coal wagon I felt closer to dying than ever before.

Finally, after meandering in the mountainous Sudetenland for days on end, we stopped for good at Litomerice—only fifty miles from where we'd started in Oederan.

We were then loaded into trucks by the women SS guards and driven a short way to a huge brick fortress hundreds of years old, Theresienstadt, or Terezín in Czech. The Nazis had incarcerated the Prague Jews there beginning in 1941, and a few of the Czechs among us were now returning to their former prison. It was many things in one, they said, a ghetto, a labor camp, and a departure point for Auschwitz. There was a large crematorium, they added, but it was mainly used to burn the bodies of inmates who had died of natural causes; Theresienstadt was not a death camp. What they did not know was that a gas chamber had recently been constructed in a secret passageway in the fortifications.

The killing apparatus was probably intended to finish off Jews like us who were still alive at the war's end, but it was never used. About the time I arrived, the camp had been taken over by the International Red Cross as part of a deal worked out with the Commandant, SS Colonel Karl Rahm. As is well known, a year and a half earlier, a Red Cross delegation had visited Theresienstadt and been fooled by the Nazis into thinking it was a "model camp," offering recreation to its residents. But now the human misery was unmistakable and the Germans were in no position to foil the relief effort.

Rahm and some of his henchmen would remain for a while, but they spent their time dismantling the gas chamber and burning incriminating documents. They no longer exercised any power. Once that became clear, the female SS guards who had brought their human freight from Oederan fled into the countryside. In its final stage, the camp would be run by devoted teams of doctors, nurses, and orderlies, including some concentration camp survivors.

My friends and I were half dead upon arrival, so thin and thirsty, so weak and weary, that we barely realized our five and a half years of torture were over. A nurse weighed me soon after I entered the camp; she reported I was twenty-nine and a half kilograms, or sixty-five pounds.

In Theresienstadt we were revived in a huge infirmary and convalescence unit that would eventually house over fifteen thousand emaciated Jews from concentration camps all over Europe. Many, like me, had made the journey in coal wagons, others came by truck, and still others had been force-marched.

Some had brought in typhus. It was discovered soon after we arrived, and it spread rapidly not only among the newcomers but also the 30,000 long-term inmates. Every day in early May, about a hundred people died from the disease and roughly a hundred new cases were diagnosed.

Every asset and every able-bodied person was needed to fight the plague. Regina and I had perked up with fluids, vitamins, and canned food—we knew not to eat too much, too fast—and were ready to assist the medical staff. Because she and I had had typhus in the ghetto only a few years earlier, we were immune and not worried about contagion. We thought of our family members who could now be suffering from infectious diseases anywhere in Europe; we hoped that they'd have healthy people trying to help them too.

We now entered the newly established quarantine zone, including barracks and some open land, set apart from the rest of the camp by a wire fence. Within that area, we who were not infected had separate sleeping and dining quarters, but because we worked among the typhus patients we were required to remain in quarantine. Manya and Franya, who were vulnerable to the disease, stayed outside.

In addition to inmates who volunteered, like Regina and me, an outpouring of support came from the surrounding community. An organization called Czech Assistance Action sent hundreds of medical personnel to Theresienstadt, caregivers who put their own health at risk to save others. It was characteristic of the compassion shown by the Czech people to the survivors.

Regina and I worked closely with a young non-Jewish Czech physician who earlier had been an inmate in another concentration camp. Under his supervision, we administered drugs and performed simple medical procedures.

In our ward of about fifty, one patient in particular caught my attention. An older religious man, tossing in discomfort in his bed, was an exact double of one of my uncles, my father's oldest brother. He put me back in touch with my childhood years, the protective cocoon that now seemed like another lifetime. The man cried out to me that he was badly constipated, that he hadn't had a bowel movement in many days and was about to "explode." With the doctor's approval, I gave him an enema with a device primitive by today's standards. Using a rubber hose connected to a big can, containing a watery solution, I inserted the nozzle into his rectum. No doubt, both of us would have felt a lot of embarrassment about this in prewar times, but now all that mattered was to get him back to health.

The enema worked and he was like a new person. I continued to attend to him, washing his face and combing his hair as I'd done for my dying father back in the ghetto, and the man's gratitude was boundless. Sometimes, in front of other people, he'd kiss my hand and tell me I'd saved his life. Caring for him and many others in Theresienstadt completely changed my sense of myself. Overnight I had gone from being someone despised and disposable to a person valued and needed.

Colonel Rahm and the last of the SS officers fled on May 5, 1945, and three days later the war in Europe ended. Some of the former Theresienstadt guards had put on concentration camp uniforms and tried to pass as new Jewish arrivals but they were detected and ran off as well. We no longer had anything to fear from the Germans.

When news came of the unconditional surrender, I could see through the wire fence of the quarantine area the celebration of inmates and townspeople alike. They unfurled Czech flags and uncorked wine bottles. But this was not the sort of mania that would engulf Times Square or Piccadilly Circus. In the heart of Europe, to rejoice wholeheartedly was impossible; too much had been destroyed.

Wide-bodied Soviet tanks arrived in Theresienstadt the day of victory and some of them drove triumphantly into the camp.

The five-man tank crews grinned, waved, and threw cans of food to the survivors and local Czechs, who laid garlands of tree branches on the tanks. Their uniforms and faces blackened, the weary soldiers had come a long way from Mother Russia and our hearts overflowed with gratitude for the sacrifice they'd made.

Then I noticed one of the tanks dragging something strange—a body. Looking closer, I saw a German soldier face down, his ankles tied to the back of the armored vehicle, and the rest of him scraping the ground, leaving behind a trail of flesh and blood. I couldn't tell if he were still alive.

So revenge was not long in coming. I had had wild fantasies in Auschwitz about getting even and had jumped for joy at the fiery destruction of Dresden, yet this grisly sight made me turn away. Regina, too, was appalled at yet another atrocity and one committed after the last shot had been fired. It wasn't a Nazi we saw being torn to pieces, but a human being. "Enough!" we said to one another, and, deeply shaken, went back to tend to the ill. If this day is to mean anything, we agreed tearfully, let it be the close of a long chapter of hatred and killing, not the opening of another one.

Others felt differently. The end of the war marked the beginning of a rampage of reprisal that spread throughout the Sudetenland. Here lived millions of ethnic Germans who had supported Hitler's annexation of the region in 1938, served in the *Wehrmacht*, and lorded it over their Czech neighbors for almost seven years. Now the Soviets were more than willing to facilitate the most violent retribution.

Word quickly spread around the camp: The Red Army would distribute weapons to any of us and to any Czech who wanted to shoot German soldiers or civilians, or plunder German homes or businesses. Regina and I were in quarantine and could not have participated in any case. But the very idea of such a vendetta revolted us. We sought to save life, not take life.

The Soviets quickly assumed command of Thereseinstadt and brought in a big, well-equipped medical team to help quell the typhus epidemic. Within a week, deaths and diagnoses of the illness had dropped sharply. But it came at a price: they extended the quarantine to the entire camp and would allow neither the healthy nor the sick to leave. The day of liberation had come and gone yet I was still penned in.

Regina and I continued to assist the Czech doctor, whose kindness toward me began to develop into romance. In the midst of the misery around us, in the wake of his own suffering as a political prisoner, he spoke about a future with me in his hometown in Bohemia. He wanted me to go there with him and meet his family as soon as we were released from quarantine.

I liked and respected him and once I realized he wasn't joking, felt flattered by the invitation. But I didn't consider it for a minute, and the fact that he was not Jewish was only a minor part of my decision.

Before anything else, I had to be back in touch with whatever, and whomever remained from my former existence. What had happened to Vevik, Cesia, and Feliks? What of my many aunts, uncles, and cousins? I held out no hope for my mother or mother-in-law, but maybe my brother and his wife had been saved by a miracle. My mind would be in turmoil, I was sure, until I could return to Lodz and find out who had lived and who had died.

If I could have spoken with Mameh, no doubt she would have told me I was still betrothed to my Chasidic cousin. I would not have accepted that, of course, but I did feel bound to Vevik, the love of my life before Auschwitz.

The doctor, bless his soul, understood why he could not be my mate and he also realized that even my work with the sick, satisfying as it was, could not claim my full attention either. He could see that after May 8 my mind and heart were drawn to the fence that separated us from the outside world. Every few hours I dropped what I was doing, walked up to the wire and talked to people from the other side. They had come to Theresienstadt from all over east-central Europe, anxiously inquiring about their loved ones, and we pumped them for information about ours.

Regina, always by my side, was desperately trying to find out what had happened to her two brothers. Neither of us learned anything for a few days and then I heard two young men shout through the barrier, "Anybody here from Lodz?"

We didn't know them but they told us they were Lodzers staying in Prague, only an hour away by train, and that others from Lodz were there as well. When we asked their names, they mentioned Martin Libicki (pronounced Libitzky in English), which meant nothing to us. Then they said Feliks Lubka.

Now my goal was to get to the Czech capital as soon as I was released from quarantine. The wait was frustrating; not until the final days of May did our isolation end. I had spent more than a month in quarantine, three weeks of it after VE Day.

During that period we continued to exchange information across the wire. One man whom I recognized was my former boss at the meat distribution center in the ghetto, the guy who had made a pass at my co-workers and me, but who probably had also looked the other way when we stole a little horsemeat. He was then the privileged official and I the fearful underling, but now he needed me and it was not only for news, but also for food. I obliged and passed him some canned goods through the fence. But neither of us could help the other find missing relatives. The only way to learn more would be to see for myself.

Yet after we were examined by a medical team in early June,

and finally freed, I did not depart for Prague immediately. My dear Czech doctor-friend referred me to an oral surgeon in town who removed the unsightly growth on my lip. Fortunately, it was benign. He did a good job of excising it, leaving only a tiny scar that I can see in the mirror to this day, a permanent reminder of that bittersweet springtime.

Now I said goodbye to the Czech doctor for the last time. He had wanted to accompany me to Prague but I had to decline that offer, too. I was embarking on a quest that he could not share.

Regina and I, along with Manya and Franya, boarded a railway car for the capital, my first ride in a real train since 1939. As we settled into our seats, we must have presented quite a sight to the other passengers. I still wore the winter coat I'd been issued on the way to Oederan. Sewn on the front was my concentration camp number and on the back a long cross, made of two reflective strips, so that I could easily be spotted by a searchlight if I escaped at night. No one seemed bothered by our appearance, however. We felt a little nervous without tickets or money, but I found out later that survivors traveling in Czechoslovakia at that time were usually allowed to ride free.

After the brief trip we exited from the Masaryk Station and made our way through the streets in order to register with the authorities and obtain the food and lodging we'd been told was available. Prague, the "city of a hundred spires," had not been heavily bombed and its incomparable bridges, castles, and churches, though sorely in need of cleaning, were largely intact and retained their architectural splendor. But the street-level view told a different story. There had been a fierce firefight on the ground for a week in early May and the Red Army was not able to liberate the city until the final day of the war. So my friends and I saw windows that had been shot out, corners of buildings that had been blasted away, and bullet holes everywhere. Overturned streetcars still blocked some thoroughfares. The cleanup, by civilian volunteers, was underway but there was still a lot of glass and rubble in the streets, even on the famous Wenceslas Square.

Highly visible was the Soviet military occupation, which would last for another half year. Troops in big armored vehicles and on horseback could be seen all over town. The Red Army requisitioned many public buildings and flew their flags from the rooftops. They also erected makeshift memorials, surrounded by flowers, to honor their fallen soldiers.

I began taking a closer look at our liberators, whom we'd all enthusiastically welcomed in Theresienstadt a few weeks earlier. Now, as they swaggered around Prague, they seemed crude and ignorant. We heard from local shopkeepers about Soviet soldiers wearing half a dozen wristwatches on their forearms, or drinking from toilet bowls that they thought were fountains. The occupying army was a mixed lot, including Tatars, Mongols, and other Asiatic Russians, and Prague was only one of several cradles of central European civilization now in their hands.

I had no idea that the Red Army was now raping almost every female in Berlin. But just from the way they lusted after my friends and me on the walk from the train station, we sensed that even in a land that had been victimized by the Nazis, the Soviet comrades felt entitled to have sex with any woman they chose. I think they believed it was a fair trade for having liberated us. Later I learned that they even had raped some survivors still in the concentration camps, women who were bone-thin and barely able to move.

The Czechs, by contrast, could not have been kinder. Quickly and courteously, the four of us were processed by government workers, issued decent clothing and shoes, and then directed to a grand hotel in the Old Town where we shared a room for the next few weeks. The cream-colored, six-story Hotel Paris (Pariz in Czech), an imposing structure for Prague at that time, contained almost a hundred units. Built at the turn of the century, it sported a neo-Gothic façade and Art Deco features inside. It was now filled mostly with young Jews who had been in concentration camps earlier that spring.

Regina, Manya, Franya and I went up to the reception desk, signed our names in the register, and were handed a key to a room on the fourth floor. Of course, the Paris had lost much of its charm during the long years of Depression and war. It was neither the luxury establishment it had been earlier, nor the one it would become again at the turn of the twentieth century. In 1945, the elevators were not functioning and few rooms had private toilets or baths. The curtains in the lobby were faded, the carpets frayed, and the furniture worn. None of that mattered to me in the slightest. Simply that my friends and I were staying in a *hotel* after what we'd just been through was astounding. And the freedom to come and go as you pleased was overwhelming. It would take a while to get used to it.

The four of us started walking up the long winding staircase graced with marble pillars. Who was coming down but Feliks Lubka! Another man was with him, whom he introduced as Martin Libitzky, who promptly missed a step and tumbled down a whole flight of stairs. (Later he would say that he fell head over heels for me.) We all rushed to his aid and fortunately found him more embarrassed than injured.

I now hugged Feliks whom I hadn't seen since the last days of the ghetto. He told me he was sharing a room, also on the fourth floor, with four other men, including his older brother, Sam; Martin; and two other friends. They had all been deported from Lodz to Auschwitz the previous August, but were held there only about a week before being transferred to a slave labor camp

The Paris Hotel as it appears today.

where they remained about eight months until being liberated by the Red Army. Then, like Regina, Manya, Franya, and me, they came to Prague as soon as they could, having heard that many survivors from their hometown had congregated in the welcoming Czech capital.

Feliks did not wait for me to ask about the brother and sister whom he and I had loved in the ghetto. Before I could say anything, he told me that he had learned nothing yet about what had happened to Cesia and Vevik.

The other girls and I went up to our room, located directly opposite the stairway landing. Regina and I took one of the two beds, Manya and Franya the other. The view from our window

143

was magical, like the background of a Renaissance painting. We wanted to explore this enchanting place but were even more eager to search for friends and relatives. Feliks, Martin, and the guys with them, we were sure, would help on both counts. Their room was just a few doors down the corridor from ours.

The next day we all went around downtown Prague together in a big group, making inquiries about our loved ones, taking in the sights, and trying to adjust to a completely new life. Even though I was already twenty-one, this was the first day of my youth; I had been imprisoned in one way or another since I was fifteen. Still unaware of the full extent of my loss, I already knew I would be in mourning the rest of my life. But I tried to push that away for a little while and enjoy the pleasures of Prague, and freedom, in June.

We returned to the hotel for our meals, which were delicious and plentiful, and served on china atop a tablecloth. I recall eating butter for the first time in years. Back on the street we met a few young Czechs, told them our story, and they gave us choice sweets. But information was slow in coming.

Late the next night, shortly after I returned from the bathroom down the hall, and before the four of us prepared for bed, we heard a commotion through our door. It sounded like a pack of drunken Red Army men coming up the circular staircase—for us. One or more of them must have spied us earlier.

When they reached our room, they pounded on the door. We were petrified. Was gang rape the next horror we'd have to endure, right *after* our liberation? The only way out was through the window, and along a very narrow ledge, to the window of our five new friends.

The ledge outside my hotel room as it looks today.

7 Hitler was our Matchmaker

IT TOOK ABOUT TWENTY SMALL steps to get to the outside of the guys' room. They were startled to see me at their window and hurriedly opened it. One by one, four frightened girls came in from the night.

Not a word of explanation was needed. By now the tumult had spread through the corridor and the Soviet soldiers were pounding on our friends' door, too. But this time the intruders were met by loud male voices and they quickly withdrew.

Just to be sure the danger had passed, the nine of us stayed together for the rest of the night, but the next morning we girls went back to our room. We were relieved to see that it had not been entered. We slept there for the rest of our time in Prague, knowing that a safe haven was nearby. During the days, we continued to search the city for loved ones. The Russians ignored women accompanied by men so we clung to the Jewish guys from Lodz as shields. Any woman alone was defenseless.

As we made our way through the quaint streets, Martin Libitzky, handsome and muscular, began to attach himself to me and I learned a little of his life story. He was working class, the son of a kosher butcher and himself a barber. But his real passion was gymnastics and before the war he had been a proud member of the Bar Kochba Association, Lodz's famous Jewish sports club. Eight years older than me, he had been drafted into the Polish army in 1938. When the Germans invaded the following year, he fought bravely in defense of Warsaw and Poznan but was captured and held in a POW camp until mid-1940. Then he was transferred to the Lodz ghetto where he shared a small, dilapidated apartment with eight family members on Mickiewicza Street. He worked as a fireman, a relatively good job in Rumkowski's kingdom, but the extra rations Martin brought home barely made a difference in meeting the needs of his overcrowded household.

In 1942, he looked on helplessly as both his parents starved to death; it was similar to the way I'd lost Tateh. Martin was deported to Auschwitz a week after me, on August 30, 1944,

Martin, upper right, at gymnastics before the war.

Martin's parents before the war.

when most of the police and firemen were evacuated, and only a day before Rumkowski himself suffered the same fate. Upon his arrival, the Eldest was torn limb from limb by other inmates and Martin witnessed the deadly beating. But he remained in Auschwitz only about eight days before being transported to the slave labor camp at Friedland in central Germany. Until the end of the war he worked assembling rocket propellers, toiling next to his brother and the other Lodzers now in that Prague hotel room: Feliks and Sam Lubka, Morris Zweibaum, and Leon Epstein.

Martin, the youngest in his family of five children, already suspected that two of his three sisters were dead, and he'd soon find out that the third had drowned attempting to escape to Sweden. Only one sibling was left, his much older brother, Joe, whose wife and small son had died in the ghetto. The Libitzky brothers had an aunt and uncle who had immigrated to America well before the war, but regarding the huge extended family in Poland, there was barely any hope.

Like the rest of us, Martin was numb from grief and there were long silences when he had to be alone with his thoughts. Only decades later, I'd find out a lot more, such as his marriage in the ghetto in March 1941 to a woman named Brandla Monszajn, three years younger than himself; she, too, had perished. On my part, I told Martin of my sheltered Chasidic girlhood and my suffering in the ghetto and camps, but revealed nothing about Vevik. Martin was my friend and protector but there were limits to what we confided in one another.

Overriding everything in those days was my need to know the fate of my family. But answers were hard to find because in the camps we appeared completely different from how we were in normal life or even in the ghetto. Often we were known only by a nickname or a merely a number. A survivor I questioned on the streets of Prague could have been in the same slave labor camp, even the same barrack, as one of my relatives and yet be unable to make the connection.

A few times my spirits soared only to come crashing down to earth a few moments later. I'd spot someone in the distance I was sure I recognized—a cousin, a friend. But coming closer I'd discover the person was a complete stranger. Yet within a couple of days I did find one of the people I cared most about in this world, Cesia, whom I'd last seen as we'd boarded the cattle cars to Auschwitz. I returned to the hotel early one evening and there she was waiting for me in the lobby. She had made it!

But as we kissed and hugged each other, I could tell something was very wrong. She had no news of Vevik but she seemed agitated and angry about something else. Then she blurted out that Feliks, her sweetheart in the ghetto less than a year ago, now showed little interest in her. Cesia didn't give me any reasons for his change of heart, but I could imagine: the fun-loving Feliks, now surrounded by pretty Czech women and tasting the first fruits of freedom, wanted to keep his options open. Beyond that, who could say how Auschwitz and the slave labor camp had changed him? How could Cesia expect him to be the same person?

*In Prague, Feliks the ladies man with, left to right,
a Czech girl, Regina, a reserved Cesia, and me.*

Yet during her own ordeal, she had assumed that, if they
both survived, they'd marry. Now she was hurt and humiliated.
She spent another day or two with my circle of friends, which
of course included Feliks, and when his eyes wandered toward
others you could read the pain in her face.

And then she vanished. I never saw her again, this girl who
had introduced me to modern Polish culture, who had lifted me
up in the ghetto, who had hidden with me and our mothers and
Vevik in a sweltering attic. To this day I don't know what became
of my sister-in-law.

I learned painfully that even if someone I loved survived the
war, there was no guarantee he or she would remain in my life.
Nothing could be as it was before.

I dreaded returning to my birthplace but after a week in Prague
I felt that I had to make the journey home. I remembered that in
the ghetto, whenever I had discussed with my family the prospect

of being deported and dispersed, the conversation usually ended with a pledge to reunite in Lodz after the war.

Martin, too, was ready to go back. But I declined his invitation to travel together; he went on his own and I stayed in Prague for a few more days. Joining him on such a momentous, emotional journey for both of us might have led him on more than I'd wanted.

When I finally set off for Lodz, my best friend, Regina, did not go with me either. She'd become interested in one of the men in the fourth-floor hotel room, Feliks' older, more reserved, and better-educated brother, Sam Lubka, who was also a good friend of Martin. Even so, her mind was mostly on her two brothers, whom she had reason to believe had been liberated in the Bergen-Belsen concentration camp and were still in northwestern Germany. So her goal was eventually to search for them there.

I wasn't entirely alone on the way back to Lodz, though; my

In Prague, our group poses with three Czech soldiers. Leon Epstein and a Czech girl are in the lower left. Cesia appears wistful as she places her hands on Feliks' shoulders. Regina has her arms around a Czech soldier while Martin's brother, Joe, has a hand on my shoulder.

other two roommates, Manya and Franya, boarded the train with me. But for some reason we sat in different parts of the railway car. I had a lot of time to think.

And only heading home, gazing out the train window at the scarred landscape, did I begin to confront the magnitude of the disaster and the extent of my loss. The week in Prague had been a whirl of new friends, good food, and luxurious lodging. I was like a bird let out of its cage. Even the hair-raising escape on the ledge and the bittersweet encounter with Cesia had been distractions of a sort. But now, speeding toward Lodz, I was coming closer and closer to a basic truth that overshadowed everything else: nearly all my relatives had been murdered. I became overwhelmed by feelings stronger than sorrow—a total lack of meaning or purpose. Before Auschwitz my life had revolved around my family members and I couldn't imagine a future without them.

After we crossed the border into Poland another sensation washed over me: fear for my physical safety. I was wearing the overcoat from the Oederan slave labor camp and soon realized the reflective strips on the back of that garment were like a magnet drawing hostility. People gawked at me as if I was a freak and I could almost read their minds—"We thought we already got rid of you Jews."

A young man in a Polish naval uniform soon entered my car and sat down next to me. He spoke softly, but with a note of urgency in voice. "They are attacking returning survivors," he said of his countrymen. "Go back to Czechoslovakia as soon as you can; you're in danger here." He told of Jews, including females, being thrown off moving trains and beaten on the streets.

Indeed, Poland was ravaged by anti-Semitic violence *after* the liberation, and about a thousand Jews would be killed by 1947. The Poles were disturbed to see a remnant of us improbably returning from hell and feared we'd lay claim to a house, a business, or even a Jewish child hidden among non-Jews. Stalin's placement of Jews in top positions in the emerging communist bureaucracy stoked the hatred even more, while the Catholic Church, having learned nothing from Hitler's barbaric rule, continued to preach anti-Judaism as it had before the war.

The most infamous atrocity would take place in July 1946 in the city of Kielce where a mob of Poles lynched dozens of Jews in broad daylight. But another appalling episode occurred much earlier, in early June 1945, around the time of my conversation with the Polish sailor. In the southeastern town of Rzeszow, precisely in the direction our train was heading, a rabbi and other Jewish leaders were arrested and accused of the ritual murder of a nine-year-old Catholic girl. They were eventually released but not before a pogrom that resulted in severe beatings and widespread looting.

I don't know if the Polish sailor knew of that incident when he warned me, but the alarm he sounded rang true; it reminded me of how our Polish neighbors had betrayed my father to the SS and plundered our store in September 1939.

By the time we pulled into Cracow, where Manya, Franya, and I were supposed to change trains for Lodz, I was afraid to continue as planned. The two sisters, though, insisted on going home so I tearfully parted from my friends in the busy railway station and by myself boarded a train back to the Czech capital. I wouldn't return to my homeland for almost half a century.

But it turned out that back in Prague I soon got the information I was seeking. Martin had come back from Lodz only a day earlier and brought a letter for me. He was grim as he took it out of his pocket.

I tore it open and my first reaction was sheer joy.

The writer was my older cousin Bronka. Simply to know that she was alive gave me a tremendous boost. Like me, she had been deported to Auschwitz and later transported to a slave labor camp but as I now learned, she had escaped and made her way to Lodz soon after its liberation in early 1945. She joined a relief organization, which helped returnees obtain food and shelter—and news about their relatives. Bronka was working behind the window of the registry when Martin walked up and inquired about his family. After consulting her records to answer his request, she asked him for the names of other Lodzers in Prague, and soon found out that one of them was her first cousin, me.

I read further, my hands shaking, as I learned the fate of my mother's family. Bronka's and my grandfather, the respected community leader Abraham Katz, had had four children and they and their spouses were all dead. But at least one child of each of them had survived. I was shocked to learn that Grandfather Katz's youngest daughter, my ravishing and resourceful Aunt Bronka, had died of disease at war's end. Of all my relatives, I'd thought she would be the likeliest to survive. But at least her only offspring, cousin Etta, had come out of the fire alive, as had my cousin Keinda, a daughter of my Aunt Rivke. I was the one to continue the line of my mother's branch of the Katz family. My cousin Bronka continued the line of my uncle Yankel. (Bronka didn't yet know it, but her youngest brother, Michael, was alive as well. The skinny kid whom she had taken under her wing in the ghetto, and once plucked from a transport to the Chelmno death camp, miraculously survived Auschwitz at age eighteen and was now in Italy waiting for a ship to take him to Palestine.)

But the rest of the letter was crushing. Bronka, who had occasionally stopped by our apartment in the ghetto, knew something about my relationship with Vevik and now had to inform me of the terrible outcome. Vevik was dead. She did not have to search for his name on a list. Her husband had known Vevik in the ghetto and became his closest friend after

Auschwitz, when they ended up in the same slave labor camp in Germany, Gross-Rosen, known for its brutality. They died there together. (Sixty-five years later, I uncovered the specifics: Vevik indeed perished in a sub-camp of Gross-Rosen, named Riese, but on May 22, 1945, two weeks after the war ended, while I was in quarantine in Theresienstadt. According to a document issued by the Red Cross, the complications he suffered from starvation were so serious that the Soviet liberators could not revive him. He was buried in the former place of his captivity.)

And what of my father's family, the Gerszts? Bronka couldn't know for sure, but there was no evidence that even one of my many aunts, uncles, or cousins was still alive. The Jews in outlying towns like Kalisz and Zdunska Wola were murdered at an even higher rate than were those in Lodz. I almost collapsed when I realized I was most probably the sole survivor of my father's big Chasidic clan.

Bronka concluded by cautioning me not to return to Lodz although she herself would stay on a little longer because she was providing vital social services for the survivors. But she and most of the other Jews who had straggled back to our hometown or come out of hiding—barely ten thousand out of the prewar population of a quarter million—were preparing to emigrate. Citing the persistent anti-Semitism of the Poles, and the harsh military occupation of the Soviets, she saw no future whatsoever in the land of our birth. It was a graveyard, she said. The premonition of doom I'd had on the train had proven all too true.

I put down the letter and Martin and I stared at each other. He had returned to his family's prewar home at Zeromskiego 44, he told me, and saw the furniture still there but no trace of his relatives. This strong, athletic man wept openly in front of me. From Bronka he had learned that except for one young cousin, he and his brother had evidently lost everyone.

We didn't know each other well but were bound together by our feelings of utter desolation. And yet I had to be in my own world. I needed to absorb the meaning of Bronka's letter by myself. I am trying to absorb it still.

In a daze I went back to my room in the Paris Hotel. I couldn't speak with anyone, not even Regina. The next day, with Martin and the other guys from Lodz, Regina and I continued to wander through streets of Prague but my very existence seemed unreal. My stomach was full but my soul was empty.

Many survivors would drift like this for years. Some would never emerge from deep depression and a few committed suicide. I, too, knew that I would remain tormented forever, but my aimless interlude was brief. I was not the sort to go to pieces. Despite all that the Nazis had done to me and had taken from me, I was determined to get back on a normal path.

From where this willpower arose, I am not entirely sure. Certainly, I was sustained by the sense of personal responsibility with which I'd been raised on Napiorkowskiego Street. It meant a lot, too, that I'd found loyal, like-minded friends. We were all in the same boat; we had one another. And being a sole survivor, actually offered me some hope. Like the one seedling that had not been consumed by a massive forest fire, maybe I was spared for a reason: in order to generate new growth.

Still, it was excruciating to go on. I needed to summon almost as much strength facing the void of 1945—the heartache, the injustice, the absurdity of it all—as I did facing the torture of 1944.

Fortunately, a clear goal soon emerged. We heard that the U.S. Army was occupying a large swath of western Czechoslovakia where forces led by General George S. Patton had set up almost a dozen Displaced Persons camps. There were six of us now: Regina

and I, and four of the five guys in that fourth-floor hotel room—
Martin, Feliks, Sam, and Morris. If we could make it to the city
of Pilsen, less than a hundred kilometers west of Prague, we'd be
in the American zone, a big first step toward starting our lives
anew. From there, we thought, we could say good riddance to
the European continent. We were grateful to the Czechs for their
generosity, but the Soviet military rule there had made even that
nation unbearable.

Our march to freedom, our exodus, began in late June.
Since train travel between the Soviet and American zones was
disrupted, we had to walk a good deal of the way. We were hardly
the only ones trudging on the narrow country roads and spending the night in barns. It seemed like all of Central Europe had
been uprooted.

Finally, we entered the medieval town of Pilsen, Czechoslovakia, now an industrial hub. At a registration center we encountered a group of GIs who could not have been more different than
the Russians: they were sympathetic, courteous, and efficient.
They assigned us to a DP camp in Salzburg, Austria, now under
American occupation, but in the meantime we would be housed
in temporary barracks in Pilsen. (As it turned out, the U.S. would
abandon western Czechoslovakia to the Soviets by the end of
1945, so I see now that we took advantage of an opportunity
that didn't last long.)

Pilsen, a gateway for tens of thousands of DPs moving west-
ward that summer, was also a seedbed of Zionist activity. The
semisecret organization known as Bricha (meaning "flight" in
Hebrew) was just getting underway in Czechoslovakia. Young,
tanned *shlichim*, emissaries from Palestine, tried to persuade
us refugees to rebuild our lives in Eretz Yisrael, the only valid
response, they said, to the annihilation of European Jewry. They
promised to arrange our transportation to an Italian seaport,

from where we'd sail—illegally—to Haifa, hopefully eluding the British Royal Navy patrolling the Palestinian coast. The cocky shlichim made a compelling case for *aliyah*, and despite the peril it posed, we set ourselves the goal of reaching the Jewish homeland. If we needed direction in our lives, this was it—to be living bridges between the destruction and rebirth of our people. And Zionism provided not only an aim for the future, but also an insight about the past: Simply put, our vulnerability had flowed from our statelessness.

Palestine was also the dream of two lively sisters who joined the six of us in Pilsen, in a sense replacing Manya and Franya who were now in Lodz. Sophie and Miriam Rosenzweig had gone through hell together—the Lodz ghetto, Auschwitz, slave labor camps—and I could see that their uncommon devotion to one another must have contributed greatly to their survival.

Morris had been the first in our group to meet Sophie as she was awaiting her younger sister's arrival in the Pilsen train station. Sophie spoke so glowingly about the virtues of the eighteen-year-old Miriam that Morris thought he, too, ought to wait for her and see for himself. From a prominent religious family, he was a highly disciplined man and anything but impulsive. But as soon as Miriam stepped down from the railway car he was smitten by her girlish charms and they soon became an inseparable couple.

The more-mature Sophie, meanwhile, gravitated toward Feliks who, even as a refugee only six weeks removed from a slave labor camp, was a sharp dresser with a knack for attracting the ladies. When they came to Pilsen the two Rosenzweig sisters had no friends and were eager to join our circle. They had experienced the same horrors as the rest of us and had sustained similar loss. Miriam's twin brother, their middle sister, and an older brother had not survived. But also like us, the sisters enjoyed the diversions of DP camp life including late-night parties. They fit in perfectly.

We were now four couples: Morris and Miriam, Feliks and Sophie, Sam and Regina, and Martin and I. The men, all in their late twenties, were each considerably older than their girlfriends. We had an enormous amount in common: all eight of us were born and raised in Lodz or its environs and had endured the same ghetto and death camp. The guys had all been firemen or policemen under Rumkowski, worked side by side in the same slave labor camp, and shared a hotel room in Prague after the liberation.

Besides the budding romances, there were two sets of siblings (Feliks and Sam Lubka, and Miriam and Sophie Rosenzweig) and two sets of best friends (Martin and Sam, and Regina and I.) Obviously, we all spoke the identical dialect, big-city Polish sprinkled with a lot of Yiddish, and although I was the only former Chasid, all of us had broken with the strict religious world of our parents. More to the point, every one of us young people had to struggle with the loss of our parents in the inferno. I had been part of other surrogate families before—with Cesia, Feliks, and Vevik in the ghetto, later with my four Auschwitz sisters, and still later with Manya, Franya, and Regina in Theresienstadt and Prague. But with these seven in Pilsen I would form my strongest bonds since childhood and the longest-lasting unions of my entire life.

And yet it wasn't so simple. Life rarely is. When we got off the train in Salzburg, a city of breathtaking beauty in the shadow of the Alps, it was unclear whether Martin and I had a future together. I think he was frustrated that I didn't have the same feelings for him as he had for me. Even though he was an attractive man, and a good soul, I didn't feel the same passion for him that I'd had for Vevik. So Martin left the other seven of us in Salzburg to meet up with his brother, Joe, and travel to Germany where they'd try their luck on the black market, already in full swing throughout central Europe. I didn't know whether I'd ever see him again.

I now spent a lot of time with Feliks, always like a brother to me. Conditions in the DP camp in Salzburg were still primitive in mid-1945, and our group was housed in one big barrack with many other refugees, male and female. The food was also inadequate so he and I went into the surrounding countryside to ask for fruit, vegetables, and eggs. When farmers weren't generous, we'd sneak into their barns and help ourselves.

We felt we needed to move on, but in Salzburg, with better access to world news, our zeal for aliyah began to cool. We had hoped that after the war Prime Minister Churchill would lift the hated White Paper and admit Jewish refugees to Palestine. President Truman, sympathetic to our plight, urged him to accept 100,000 survivors immediately. But Churchill was unexpectedly voted out of office in July 1945 and the new British government continued to enforce its cruel policy. At the same time, bloodshed inside the Holy Land intensified as extremist Jewish groups such as the Irgun and Stern Gang blew up British targets. In Salzburg, our group of seven all remained staunch Zionists and still seriously considered aliyah, but we were not prepared to leave immediately with the Bricha for Italy in order to face British destroyers in the Mediterranean and British troops in Palestine. Feliks in particular opposed the idea of going from one war to another and we all agreed with him.

Meanwhile, the American authorities offered us a temporary alternative. A large, well-equipped DP camp, Foehrenwald, had just opened across the Austrian border in Bavaria. The thought of being in Germany was more than we could stomach, of course, but we thought this camp, already in the international spotlight, would be our springboard out of Europe. I couldn't imagine that the major world powers would waver much longer on the humanitarian crisis of a quarter million Jewish DPs, most of them now stuck in the house of the hangman. But in fact the delay took over three and a half years. I wouldn't get out of Germany until 1949.

Fortunately, Foehrenwald was one of the most desirable of the many dozens of DP camps in Germany and Austria. A very young American social worker named Henry Cohen, attached to the U.S. Army, ran the place with competence and dedication. Holding about 5,000 Jews, it was a self-contained community with its own schools and synagogues, police force and fire brigade, post office and hospital. There were cultural and recreational activities day and night. The camp even published its own Yiddish newspaper, *Bamidmar*, or "In the wilderness," which not only carried news about Foehrenwald, but also informed us of the struggle for Palestine and the debates in Washington. It was indeed, a period in the wilderness, suspended between slavery and the Promised Land. We were liberated, but not yet free. In the meantime, we tried to enjoy the creature comforts we'd been denied for so long. We ate well and drank a lot, played cards and

A Zionist youth group dances the "Horah" in the Foehrenwald Displaced Persons Camp, 1945. (courtesy USHMM)

listened to music, and most of all took pleasure in each other's company. It felt like being on vacation.

Of course even the best DP camps had their problems and at times Foehrenwald was plagued by floods, power failures, and even a brief typhus epidemic. Worse than any physical discomfort was the mounting frustration with the international foot-dragging over the predicament of us refugees. One way to let off steam was through noisy rallies and demonstrations and these occurred almost every month. But restless DPs sometimes went further and tangled with GIs in the camp and with local cops in the nearby town Wolfratshausen. One time the German police shot and killed a DP in Wolfratshausen and violence erupted at his funeral.

But overall, I remember an atmosphere of healing and hope as people began to rebuild their shattered lives. The wooded, mountain setting was soothing in itself. Before the war Foehrenwald had housed employees of the vast chemical concern, I.G.

Street scene in Foehrenwald, 1945. (courtesy USHMM)

Farben; workers and their families had lived in cute little brick cottages on tree-lined pathways. Our group of seven was able to get a two-bedroom bungalow just for ourselves on recently named Indiana Street. You could say we had our own little commune, with three couples each sharing a bed, and me sleeping alone. I had a few suitors in Foehrenwald—pairing up was on everyone's mind—but somehow I stayed single. The seven of us ate our meals together and went out in the evenings together. The men began dabbling in the black market together and pooled their gains.

Outside the circle of Lodzers, I befriended one couple coincidentally also named Sam and Regina. Sam Spiegel of Kozienice and his close companion, Regina Gutman of Radom, both very bright and personable, had met and actually fallen in love in a slave labor camp. They were later sent to Auschwitz where of course they were separated, but after the war they were reunited and would marry during their stay in Foehrenwald. They had been among the first DPs in the camp and showed me the ropes. But of course my survival skills were quite well honed by that time and when our group needed some extra edibles, I knew how to smuggle food out of the storage bins by concealing it under a loose-fitting pair of pants.

Sam invited me to join him in a critical project in those early days: establishing a registry as my cousin Bronka had done in post-liberation Lodz. Dozens of new people were coming into Foehrenwald every week and many had vital information about missing persons. I couldn't think of anything more vital than recording and organizing that data and eventually the camp administration agreed; they turned over our work to their professional staff.

I now had more time on my own but that did not last long. One fall day, with no notice, Martin and Joe Libitzky showed up. The older brother would soon return to Czechoslovakia and marry a gorgeous Czech woman he had been courting. But Martin moved right into our little house and stayed. He had missed our whole group and me more than he could say.

I still had doubts but, when he pursued me this time, we became lovers. Obviously there was a practical reason: the other seven were waiting for me to find a guy and he completed our group as no one else could. The men were his best buddies, the women already well known to him. Beyond that, he provided me with a lot of security. He had already saved me from Red Army men intent on rape and protected me on the trek from Prague to Pilsen. Even though I was now well out of the range of the Soviets, I knew that a young woman alone anywhere in Europe during that chaotic period was highly vulnerable. Weighing on me heaviest, however, was the loneliness I'd felt since coming back to Prague after my abortive trip to Lodz. I was sure that Martin loved me deeply and I desperately craved the intimacy that would come with giving myself to him.

Of course, earlier in my life it was unimaginable that I would be living with a man out of wedlock, and in a house with three other unmarried couples. But the only approval I needed was that of my friends—they were all that mattered now—and this was the arrangement they'd already chosen for themselves.

Yet it didn't stay that way for long because we all wanted to start families. Soon after the turn of the year, we eight were sitting in our cottage when we looked at one another and got the idea at roughly the same time: a quadruple wedding—all four couples would marry one after the other under the same *chuppah*. We set the date for Saturday night, January 26, 1946.

Even though we didn't print any invitations, word got out and hundreds of people attended, many from other DP camps. In fact, we turned our own cottage over to out-of-town guests and spent our wedding night sleeping on straw in an attic. In Wolfratshausen we rented four similar white wedding dresses and on the roaring black market in Munich the guys obtained large quantities of hard liquor and delicious pastries. A nearby farmer slaughtered a whole cow along with dozens of chickens for us. Even we brides had too much to drink and had to walk it off outside in the freezing Bavarian night. But the celebration continued for a whole week. Our marriage was a grand occasion that cheered everyone—a slap in Hitler's face and a bet on the future of the Jewish people.

An Orthodox Hungarian rabbi hand-wrote in Hebrew the four *ketubot*, or marriage contracts. Neither Martin nor I disclosed our former marriages to the rabbi or to one another; I went to the altar as Chava Gerszt. I'd always felt more of a personal commitment than a legal bond to Vevik and now that he was dead, I didn't feel the piece of paper, signed by Rumkowski in such an abnormal situation, was still valid. My real wedding was in Foehrenwald, I felt, and I considered it my first.

Before the ceremony, the rabbi's wife, the *rebbitzin*, took the four brides to the mikvah and instructed us in the laws of ritual purity. Even though we weren't religious anymore, the age-old

Our wedding picture, January 26, 1946, and the four brides.

Jewish wedding traditions on German soil, so soon after the catastrophe, aroused a lot of emotion in us.

But who would lead us down the aisle? Martin had his brother, Joe, but who would stand in for my parents? According to custom, it had to be someone who'd already been married. A friend of mine in the camp was with her mother, a middle-aged widow from Lodz, who had been kind to me since I'd arrived in Foehrenwald. I asked her to do the honor of giving me away to Martin and she accepted. There weren't many of her generation who had survived.

Martin and I were married first, then Sam and Regina Lubka. In a touching gesture, Sophie made sure that she and Feliks would be next, before Miriam and Morris, because once she was married, she could walk her beloved younger sister down the aisle a few minutes later.

Rabbi Isaac Herzog welcomed by DPs at Neu Freimann, a camp near Foehrenwald, April 1946. (courtesy USHMM)

And then a celebrity walked in, the scholarly, white-bearded Yitzchak Herzog, an Irishman who was Chief Ashkenazi rabbi of Palestine (and the father of Chaim Herzog, a future president of Israel). He had been visiting DP camps in Germany and heard about our unusual four-part wedding but he arrived late, when the ceremony was almost over. He did participate, however, in blessing the last couple, Miriam and Morris.

Naturally, my joy that night was mixed with melancholy. I had not one relative present.

If it hadn't been for the war, my family would have rejoiced at my marriage, at age sixteen, to my first cousin and I might have had several children by now at age twenty-one. Of course, I might have been unhappy, I might have chafed under all the restrictions, but that was the life for which my childhood had prepared me.

How I'd been tossed about by the upheavals of my time! Even after I was plunged into the secular world, the man I fell in love with and married in the ghetto was torn away from me and killed by Nazis. I knew that had Vevik lived, there was no guarantee we would have even remained together, much less had a good marriage; the example of Feliks and Cesia showed me how things could change. But there was no denying that once again my life-plan had been wrecked. I wouldn't be with the husband my father chose for me, and I also wouldn't be with the husband I chose.

I was now wedded to another man, whom I would gradually come to love, but he was not someone I would have married under normal circumstances, even in the non-religious world. Others in our circle also realized that they and their spouses had been thrown together by outside forces, and had bonded more out of necessity than choice. "Hitler was our matchmaker" was a phrase we said often in the years to come.

8 In Limbo

Like almost all DPs, we took part in the black market and raised our standard of living markedly. The economics were simple: Organizations like UNRAA (the United Nations Relief and Rehabilitation Administration) and the JDC (American Jewish Joint Distribution Committee) distributed ample quantities of coffee, chocolate, and cigarettes to DPs and we could easily obtain more from the GIs who policed the camp. But these luxury items, and even staples like fruit, tea, milk, and sugar, were in very short supply among the German public, whose provisions were strictly rationed by the Allied authorities. To get the goods they craved—or in some cases were addicted to—the Germans had to barter their clothing, furniture, housewares, and even their watches, cameras, and jewelry. The recently defeated "master race" was sullen and, especially in Bavaria, still anti-Semitic, but trading us their prized personal possessions on the black market was their only option.

Of course I thought back to my days in the ghetto when Tateh had been forced to exchange one of my mother's diamond rings for a loaf of bread. Now the tables were turned, and we all saw at least a tiny bit of justice in the new situation. It was like reparations before there were reparations.

Our four husbands worked as a team. They not only traveled to nearby Wolfratshausen but also further afield to Munich and Frankfurt, occasionally taking riskier trips to Prague and Berlin. The intensity of operating outside the law sometimes caused the guys to quarrel, and I heard insults like "idiot," "coward," and "gonif," but they always patched things up and frequently brought home treasures. Once, for four cartons of cigarettes, I got a numbered antique gold-leaf tea service from Silesia; it had probably belonged to a Jewish family before the war and I felt I deserved it more than did some German. Another time, a bag of groceries bought me an old-fashioned twelve-piece silver dinner set. By coincidence, it was already engraved with my husband's initials, ML.

For all of that, we were small-timers. Other DPs illegally speculated in foreign currency or precious metals and reaped huge profits that they deposited in secret Swiss bank accounts. Those fortunes later enabled them to start legitimate businesses or buy real estate in the United States or elsewhere. Although my brother-in-law managed to leave Germany with a couple of thousand dollars from black market activities, no one in my circle of friends ended up with anything close to that amount. It wasn't for lack of trying, but rather that the guys just weren't good smugglers. One time they were on a train bringing a suitcase full of fresh oranges—a great delicacy—to trade in Czechoslovakia. Somehow the valise came open and the oranges fell out and rolled all over the railway car. Many of the other passengers got an unexpected treat.

Our group in Foehrenwald with Martin's bother, Joe, at the top in the center. From left to right, Miriam, myself, Regina, and Sophie, Morris, Martin, Sam, and Feliks.

Such madcap scenes were part of the unnatural life we led—engaged in a shady enterprise and not holding real jobs. We were also free of the obligations that come with raising kids.

But that began to change during 1946 as many of us newly married women got pregnant and delivered babies.

The DP camps, in fact, soon had one of the highest birth rates in the world. The first couple in our group to have a baby was Miriam and Morris, whose son Steven was born in August. By then Sophie was pregnant and so was I. Bringing forth new life is almost always exhilarating, but the elation of childbirth in the DP camps was in a category all by itself. The large majority of new mothers had been malnourished slave laborers or death-camp inmates only a couple of years earlier. Most had not menstruated during that time and feared that, even if they survived, they would never be able to conceive a child. But defying all of that, we were now starting a new generation that would carry the names of our murdered parents and ensure the continuity of the Jewish people.

Yet I wasn't certain we were psychologically ready to be mothers. Having been so severely and so recently traumatized, could we now properly meet the needs of our babies? At first, I pushed away such fears. When a German doctor told me that we needed therapy rather than motherhood, I flew into a rage. After having been treated as less than human for six years, did he now want us to give up the chance to walk around with big bellies and feel fully feminine? But years later I saw his point. The demands of handling a newborn were overwhelming and, while I had several dear friends nearby, I sorely missed my mother or even an aunt to help me through the trying times. It was our fate

Celebrating the wedding of Sam and Regina Spiegel in Foehrenwald. Martin and I are in the lower left (I'm about six months pregnant), Sam and Regina Lubka to the right of us. The bride and groom are at the head of the table. Feliks is in the upper right.

to nurture the young in the absence of the old and I felt a terrible void. Some of the kids born to us survivors would later hear from their schoolmates the words "grandma" and "grandpa" and not even know their meaning.

In the late fall of 1946, when I was about seven months pregnant, Martin and I decided to leave Foehrenwald for the more normal environment of a small town named Bad Nauheim, near Frankfurt. Even earlier, Sophie and Feliks, also expecting a child and preferring more privacy and a less institutional setting, left the DP camp for an apartment in Stuttgart. Regina and Sam Lubka were able to get to the States by 1946; her younger brother, who had survived Bergen-Belsen, had come over on a youth transport and she, her husband, and her older brother had been granted visas to reunite with him. Miriam and Morris, their hearts set on Palestine at the time, remained in Foehrenwald.

So each of the four couples who had been married under the same *chuppah* that winter night was now on its own. But the year in the DP camp that the eight of us spent together, the year we reentered the civilized world, had already served to cement us as a family. We were apart for the time being, but we were all destined to be together again for the long run. I would think of them as my brothers and sisters; later my children would call them aunt and uncle.

In Bad Nauheim, a quiet, picturesque town known for its curative salt springs, Martin and I were given a large comfortable room in a hotel at Karlstrasse 31, which the American authorities had turned over completely to DPs. Food and clothing were dispensed by UNRAA and the JDC just as in Foehrenwald. We shared a bathroom with another expectant couple and partitioned and remodeled it to create a little kitchen. I also had a gas burner in our room so I could prepare some good meals. My chicken soup and cheesecake helped us make friends with a number of Jewish GIs, including some officers, who had picked up some Yiddish from their parents. I'd lean out our second-floor window to talk with them and, as they smelled the aroma, they'd want to know what was cooking.

If we just had a hunch that a soldier was Jewish, we'd try the password *amcha*, a well-known Hebrew term meaning people, or folk, and it usually brought a warm smile of kinship. The atmosphere in Bad Nauheim was *haimish*, or homey, and if we had to bide our time somewhere in Germany—now necessitated by my pregnancy as much as the delay in Washington and London— this seemed as good a spot as any.

Bad Nauheim had been glowingly recommended to us by Martin's only surviving cousin, Henry Rotman, who had been living there alone for a few months in a nice villa. Henry, who was my age, admired his older cousin whom he remembered from prewar Lodz as a strapping sportsman, a polished soldier, and a tough Jew who stood up to the anti-Semites. I later learned from Henry about some of my husband's prewar exploits. In the 1930s, he and his friends sometimes disguised themselves as Chasidim and if Polish hooligans harassed them, they'd hit back with brass knuckles. Later, in the Polish army, Martin had to do time in the brig for decking a fellow soldier who had shouted some vicious anti-Jewish slurs.

Henry clearly wanted Martin as a partner in black market activities and assured us that I'd receive good natal care in Bad Nauhem. Indeed, I had a distinguished obstetrician, who was glad to treat me for little more compensation than a hearty meal and some chocolate every time he made a house call.

Our son was born on January 29, 1947. I was confined to the local hospital for a week and a half (customary for new mothers in those days) and even missed the bris. But I felt more triumphant than at any time in my life. This was my way of defying Hitler.

Martin actually missed the birth—he was at a card game that night and detained by a snowstorm—but when he finally came into my hospital room, he presented me with a diamond wedding ring. He had obtained it on the black market for about ten kilos of green, unroasted coffee. I was thrilled with that gift, which replaced the plain gold band I'd worn since our wedding in Foehrenwald.

But coming home, I was deeply disappointed that Martin had not named the baby after my beloved father, Shlomo, but rather after his own father, Moishe. Coincidentally, Moishe was the name of my only sibling, the uncle our son could never know, but even so I had wanted—and expected—him to be named for my father. Yet Shlomo would only be his middle name.

Our full-time nanny, the reliable Schwester Zelma, or Nurse Zelma, an elderly German spinster, sensed the friction between Martin and me over the baby's name. She came up with a neutral alternative that was, unsurprisingly, German and not Hebrew. Schwester Zelma dubbed our boy Richard (as in Richard Strauss

Schwester Zelma and Moses.

or Richard Wagner) and somehow it stuck. That's how everyone, including us, called him, although we gave it the English rather than German pronunciation. Remarkably, he would keep that name for more than twenty years before switching to the official Moses. I wish his nickname would have been Sol instead; the name Richard held no meaning for me.

In the late winter of 1947, when Moses was about five weeks old, we thought our immigration visas for the States were about to come through. Palestine had long ceased to be our first choice as spectacular acts of violence such as the bombing of the King David Hotel occurred throughout 1946 and the British contin-ued to interdict at sea many potential Jewish immigrants and detain them behind barbed wire in Cyprus. With the safety of my baby uppermost in my mind, I set my sights on America instead. Besides, Martin had some relatives there—we had no one in Palestine—and, most important, Sam and Regina Lubka had preceded us.

But at the last minute the U.S. consulate in Frankfurt notified us of an indefinite delay. Congress would not allow more than a small trickle of Polish Jews to be admitted that year. We were let down, of course, but with an infant in my care I was content to stay put in Bad Nauheim a while longer.

And then something happened that nearly ruined our lives.

It began with the arrest of my husband right before my eyes. Late one summer evening, as we were exiting the small cinema in town, two plain-clothes Americans swooped down on us, grabbed Martin, and whisked him away in an unmarked car.

I ran after them for awhile but soon saw there was nothing I could do and returned to Schwester Zelma and my baby, then about six months old. I said goodnight to the nanny as usual and made up some excuse about Martin's absence, while my heart raced from fright and astonishment. How could he have been seized like that? I assumed it was related to the black market but I didn't know how. I couldn't even reach Henry Rotman who was out of town on a long "business trip" of his own.

I barely slept that night and at dawn, with Moses' cries loud in my ears, began to face the crisis. Should I go to the U.S. military headquarters and inquire about Martin, or approach one of the Jewish GIs we knew? Should I send a message to our close friends living elsewhere in Germany, or notify my brother-in-law in Czechoslovakia? Should I enlist the help of one of the UNRAA or JDC social workers, or retain my own lawyer? As I gathered my thoughts early that morning, a car drove up to my building. Two large men in business suits got out. It was the Americans again and this time they were coming for me.

They waited in our place until Schwester Zelma arrived to care for Moses, then hustled me out the door and drove me to an office across town. There they motioned for me to sit down across from them on a hard metal chair. Because I spoke only a few words of English, they brought in a German interpreter who grilled me in that language, bringing back a flood of horrible memories.

My interrogators identified themselves as detectives with the CID, the Criminal Investigation Division of the U.S. Army. Your husband is in serious trouble, they stated, and he is facing a prison sentence. They revealed nothing more but demanded that I tell them every detail I knew about his black market dealings.

I couldn't believe this was happening. Although I knew little about his activities, I was virtually certain he was no kingpin. True, I was aware that he and Henry had smuggled cartons of cigarettes into the British zone and that they'd had some close calls at border checkpoints. I'd heard them speak with awe about the skills of their one-legged German driver, reputedly the former chauffeur of a Nazi bigwig, who now, on behalf of two Polish

Jews, could out-maneuver any police vehicle.

But I'd always urged Martin to operate on a small scale and I thought he'd taken my advice. I'd never seen piles of cash or valuables in our home and whatever his dealings, they certainly weren't making us rich. In any case I'd assumed the U.S. authorities were fairly lax about the DPs' illicit trading. I had rarely heard of a punishment worse than confiscation of the illegal goods, a hefty fine or, if one was very unlucky, a few nights in jail.

But clearly this was not a typical black market infraction. The investigators bombarded me with questions for many hours; it was almost an inquisition. I had nothing to give them and in turn they refused to let me visit Martin or even tell me where he was being held.

When they finally allowed me to go home, I was more distraught than ever, but soon I got some answers. Around midnight, the door opened. It was Martin. He'd escaped from custody.

He explained that he'd been in jail the night before and was booked in the morning, probably around the time I was being interrogated. After he was photographed and fingerprinted—as he spoke I saw his fingers still smudged with ink—he noticed that a door down the corridor seemed to be ajar. He asked to go to the bathroom to wash his hands, and was given permission, but instead ducked out of the building, and got safely off the military base. He'd lain low all day and now needed to pack some things before fleeing Bad Nauheim, where he figured the army was already searching for him. A good friend, a Lodzer named Romek, was waiting outside to drive him to another city, he said. There was no time to waste.

What had he done to land himself and his young family in such a fix? He told me that the crime reached all the way up to a U.S. general who wanted a full-length mink coat for his wife and tried to obtain it on the black market. A go-between recruited

Martin to pull this off, and with the help of a young German woman who worked in the PX, he was able to amass hundreds of cartons of cigarettes to exchange for the prized fur. But the middleman turned out to be an undercover agent and the whole plot became known to the authorities. Because a general was implicated, the case was turned over to the Criminal Investigation Division, charged with rooting out high-level corruption across American-occupied Germany.

Martin would be on the run for nearly a year, moving from one hideout to another throughout the Allied zone. For much of that time he was in Stuttgart with Feliks and Sophie. Almost all the communication he and I had went through trusted third parties, who were passing through Bad Nauheim. I saw him only one time, when he took the risk of coming home on Moses' first birthday; the toddler, well taught by Schwester Zelma, recited a German poem for his father. But it was too dangerous for us to remain together as a family for more than a few hours.

During Martin's long absence I had a lot of support from my friends. Sophie visited from Stuttgart and brought along her baby, Sarah, born ten days after Moses. Sarah caused her mother a lot of worry by refusing to eat but fortunately a persistent Schwester Zelma was able to feed her. My baby, meanwhile, was sickly almost from the time he came out of the womb, so both the headaches and joys of caring for him preoccupied me while Martin was away. Moses suffered from respiratory ailments like asthma, and was also prone to a range of skin diseases. Just before Martin was arrested, our son was stricken with painful stomach cramps accompanied by high fever and diarrhea. The doctor suspected typhus and ordered him hospitalized. We might have lost him had it not been for a top German pediatrician who, like our OB-GYN doctor earlier, treated Moses in exchange for nothing more than some extra food.

But even when our son was well, I was filled with anxiety about my family's situation.

Never did it enter my mind that Martin would willingly abandon us. I could tell that his love for Moses and me was unshakeable. But how long would we be kept apart because of the manhunt waged by the authorities? And how could we ever be admitted to the States in light of his criminal past and flight from prosecution?

I had to try to reunite my family and immigrate to America. My lonely struggle sometimes seemed hopeless, but I told myself that I had prevailed against long odds before.

I decided to entrust everything to a young U.S. Army officer whom Martin and I had befriended long before my husband's arrest. He was born of East European Jews, and when he learned our life stories, I think he imagined what his own fate might have been had his parents not immigrated to the States early in the century. We invited him over for dinner several times and the traditional dishes he ate and the Yiddish expressions he heard reminded him of home. We laughed a lot, but we cried sometimes, too.

At one point we presented him with an unusual gift. We owned an adorable purebred German shepherd (our love for animals outweighed any associations with the Nazis using that breed) but the dog annoyed us by constantly climbing all over my pregnant body and hopping into our bed at night. So we gave him away to our American friend, who was grateful to get such a well-groomed and well-trained canine.

After Martin was underground for awhile, and with no end to our separation in sight, I had to put our friendship with the officer to the test. I needed him to look into my husband's case, give me an honest opinion about what we were up against, and possibly try to affect the outcome. It was a huge favor to ask, I knew.

Thankfully, he agreed to help, and in exchange for nothing beyond some more home-cooked meals. As a young woman without a man around, I'd had to fend off a number of GIs, but this one never tried to take advantage of me.

I don't know how he penetrated the files of the CID, but the information he retrieved gave me hope. He told me that, for political reasons, it was uncertain whether the army would actually go ahead with the prosecution. Reports of rampant wrongdoing among U.S. military personnel in occupied Germany had reached the halls of Congress, and the Pentagon was afraid of being embarrassed by another major scandal, this time involving a general. The inside story was that the whole mess might be swept under the rug. Perhaps that explained why Martin had been able to escape so easily the morning after his capture. Maybe the army wasn't that sorry to see the general's accomplice vanish. Without my husband's testimony, the prosecution would not be able to build a proper case.

Finally, my Jewish officer-friend brought back the news I'd been longing to hear. The charges had been dropped. On top of that, he had double-checked to ensure that any mention of Martin, including his arrest and flight, was expunged from the record. It was as if the whole episode had never happened. Only a short time earlier I had been mentally preparing to immigrate to Palestine or Australia, neither one a bad alternative but certainly not ideal. Now, thanks to my guardian angel in uniform, America seemed within our grasp once again.

Through his friend Romek, I got word to Martin. He moved back to our apartment in the early summer, around the time Congress passed the Displaced Persons Act of 1948, allowing tens of thousands of East European Jewish refugees to go to the head of the immigration line. My family had a good chance to get three of those places, especially after a packet arrived from Regina Lubka,

Our family in Bad Nauheim.

now settled in Hartford, Connecticut. Her younger brother, Julius Jacobs (this was now the Jakobowitz family name) was working as a meatpacker in that city and, at his request, the company formally offered Martin a similar job. Enclosed, too, were affidavits from Sam and Regina attesting to our good character and declaring that if we were admitted to the United States, we would be unlikely ever to be on the welfare rolls.

We took these documents to the American consulate and found out that we still didn't qualify though thankfully it had nothing to do with Martin's disaster on the black market. The problem this time was that we'd never recorded our marriage in Foehrenwald with the civil authorities, and the consular officials wouldn't recognize our Hebrew ketubah. So we quickly got married again by a German justice of the peace, my third "wedding" in five years, and Martin had to formally adopt Moses since I'd entered into this civil marriage with a two-year-old child in tow. Finally, our immigration visas could be issued.

We were scheduled to embark in February. Sam and Regina helped Feliks and Sophie and their daughter get visas around that time, too. We would come to America on the same ship.

Schwester Zelma cried when we said goodbye. She loved Moses deeply and was also fond of Martin and me. That trustworthy lady was one of the very few Germans I got to know well during my long stay, and I would never forget her. She was not the first German who proved to me that not everyone in that nation was evil, but it was good to be reminded. We left her our furniture and took along some pots and pans, a few ceramic figurines, and a Leica camera. We had a couple of fine antiques, too. But for all of the distress the black market had caused us, we had managed to squirrel away only $50 in cash.

We were to sail from the North Sea port of Bremerhaven. For more than a week we were put up in an emigrant dormitory, a converted warehouse, a few miles to the south in Bremen. We slept on cots, but I didn't mind the uncomfortable wait—it was a hopeful, upbeat time as I envisioned my family's new life in the Golden Land—but just before departure, misfortune came again and I thought we'd have to cancel our plans.

The final hurdle was a thorough medical examination in Bremen since we wouldn't be allowed to board the ship without a doctor's certificate affirming our good health. Forty-eight hours before the check-up, little Moses came down with an awful case of whooping cough. He emitted loud, choking sounds from deep in his throat, causing many of the other young families in the dormitory to get up and move away from us. Some of the mothers even cursed me for exposing them and their children to such a contagious toddler. Others tried to be helpful by suggesting various remedies—one claimed that smoke from a bonfire would be beneficial—but I had little hope that he'd be cured before the exam.

My journey east from Theresienstadt and then west from Cracow, 1945-49.

Even though Moses had been in good shape when we left Bad Nauheim, considering his medical track record I was not altogether surprised when he got sick in Bremen. But the timing was terrible. Given my child's illnesses, my husband's past, and Congress's whims, I thought this opportunity to immigrate to America might never come again. Once more, I was in need of a scheme.

Luckily, one sprang to mind. Waiting with us was a young couple who had been our next-door neighbors in the Karlstrasse hotel, the family with whom we'd shared our bathroom and makeshift kitchen. They too had a little boy, almost the same age as Moses and with similar long, blonde curls. Best of all, we two

Moese, on the right, and his double.

families had spent a lot of time together and her kid was very familiar with me; I'd often held him in my arms.When the time for the exam came, these warmhearted folks, at no small risk to themselves, let me take their son through the battery of tests as though he were mine. The healthy child had gone through the crowded line earlier in the day with his real mother, but none of the overworked doctors or nurses realized they were examining him for the second time. It all went smoothly and he received a pass signed by the chief physician.

I came aboard the ship holding Moses with one hand and his medical clearance with the other. I can't remember if he coughed as we went up the gangplank. The one thing I do recall is that as soon as we reached the open sea, his lungs cleared and all three of us breathed easier.

9 Down on the Farm

WE SAILED ON THE *SS Marine Shark*, built during the war as a troop carrier and now converted into a passenger ship. Somehow it lacked the stabilizers, fins mounted below the waterline of most ocean liners to counteract the roll of the waves. As soon as we were hit by a late winter storm, the vessel bobbed up and down like a toy boat. When Martin, Moses, and I went out on the deck for a meal, the table and everything on it went flying.

Before long everyone on board started retching from seasickness, everyone but a chipper Feliks who seemed immune from nausea and appeared to be enjoying the cruise. Men and women were berthed separately, and Martin and Moses spent a lot of time in their cabin, the floor a pool of vomit. I preferred to throw up over the railing on the side of the deck. Smoother sailing gave us some relief from time to time, but overall the two-week voyage was dreadful. Yet the minute we came ashore, on March 3, 1949, we all felt 100%; I kissed the ground, overjoyed to be out of Germany, in the USA—and on dry land.

Because of the elaborate screening we'd undergone in Bremen, we did not go through Ellis Island and I barely recall the Statue of Liberty. I do remember Martin's relatives, his widowed aunt, and his uncle with his second wife, meeting us on the docks and driving us across the city to the aunt's apartment in the rough neighborhood of Brownsville, Brooklyn. Her place, on Pitkin Avenue, was drab and depressing and we stayed for only a few days. Martin's American kin asked about our experiences in Europe but they were not inclined to understand what we'd been through. I wanted to leave New York as soon as I could. All I thought about was Hartford, Connecticut, where my closest friends were waiting for me and where Martin was due to start work.

We made that trip by train in a few hours and were taken in by Regina and Sam Lubka, who now had a newborn girl, Ruth. The Lubkas had been in Hartford more than a year and were living with Regina's brothers Julius and Fred Jacobs, and Fred's wife. Already there as guests were our former shipmates Feliks, Sophie, and their baby, who had come to Connecticut after a cold encounter with his snobbish American aunt in Yonkers. Adding yet another couple and a toddler made for close quarters but of course they welcomed us warmly. It meant the world for me to be reunited with Regina after more than two years. In the Lubkas' home I met a twenty-year-old visitor named David Chase, a close friend of young Julius who had come over on the same ship with him. David was destined to become one of the leading real estate developers in the Northeast, but that lay far in the future. For now, he was selling household items door to door, starting at the bottom like the rest of us.

There was no time to lose. The very day after we arrived, Martin got up early to go to work at the Union Meat Company and

I went out searching for an apartment. I got a lot of doors shut in my face, not only because I was an immigrant, literally just off the boat, but also because I had a young child.

With many veterans having returned from overseas in the past few years, apartments were scarce and property managers often demanded "key money," essentially a bribe. So when a Jewish woman offered me a furnished room with kitchen privileges, and nothing required under the table, I felt I'd better take it. I still remember the rent we paid on our first home in America—$18 a week.

That was actually a lot of money because Martin's starting salary was only $40 per week, and for that he had to put in almost eighty hours. He earned only slightly more than the minimum wage in those days, which was forty-three cents an hour. Alongside Regina's brother Julius, Martin toiled as a meatpacker for a hard-driving German Jew named Kurt Leopold, and the work was exhausting. He spent a lot of time in a giant freezer, where he needed to wear an overcoat, but as soon as he went outside with a heavy slab of beef to load on a truck, he'd break out in a sweat. Late at night he'd come home so weary and drained that all he could do was lie on the floor. Sometimes he dozed off right there.

Yet it was steady work and the boss, impressed with Martin's strength and stamina, began to raise his pay. As the son of a kosher butcher in Lodz, my husband was no stranger to this trade. But he would have taken any job, under any conditions, to support the family.

Within a few months, I found a large apartment, the upstairs of a duplex, that we could share with Feliks, Sophie, and their two-year-old, Sarah. Like us, they had been cooped up in a single furnished room after leaving Sam and Regina's. Now each family had two rooms and a kitchen and shared a bathroom. The landlord, coincidentally David Chase's employer, lived in the downstairs unit and had a TV. Moses, not yet three, sometimes watched it through the man's living room window. He pressed his little face so tightly against the wire screen that a dirty grid was impressed on his forehead.

We lived on Greenfield Street in the north end of Hartford, a neighborhood that attracted many Jews: immigrants like us, known as *grineh,* or greenhorns, as well as *Amerikaner,* meaning the native-born or those who had immigrated decades earlier. Each group went its own way when it came to synagogue life. Most of the grineh, our circle of Lodzers included, felt comfortable in the Orthodox Agudas Achim, although Martin and I did not attend often. The stately Conservative Emanuel Synagogue, with its organ and mixed seating, drew the American Jews. On the High Holidays, you could see the two different crowds socializing outside their respective shuls at either end of Greenfield Street.

Our house was directly across from sprawling Keney Park, 800 acres of trees, trails, and playgrounds. Often we'd enjoy the lovely greenery with Sam, Regina, and little Ruth, who lived nearby; with Feliks' family of course; and with Morris and Miriam Zweibaum and their son, Steven. Barely three years earlier, we eight traumatized survivors were wed in the Foehrenwald DP camp. Now we were all together in Connecticut, each couple having already brought a child into the world. We couldn't afford much more than a stroll in the park with our kids, but that in itself was a miracle.

There were other ways we entertained ourselves at little or no cost. At Sam and Regina's, we taught each other to dance by playing the same Big Band record over and over again. On Greenfield Street I also began to learn English. Because I had to stay home with Moses and couldn't attend classes, a tutor named Mrs. Katzman came to my house and instructed me in grammar and vocabulary. She taught most of my friends, too, pro bono.

After living about a year with Feliks, Sophie, and Sarah, we moved into an apartment of our own, a five-room unit in a large building on Charter Oak Avenue. It was a Polish, working class neighborhood, sprinkled with stores and factories, not far from the State Capitol. I found it by chance, looking for a place for my cousin Bronka, now Bernice. Six months after us, she immigrated to America with her husband, Mark Sobotka. Mark's first family had not survived and he started a second with Bernice, herself a widow. With their baby, Jacob, they had originally intended to settle in Pittsburgh, but I convinced them to move to Hartford where they'd be near my family and my group of former Lodzers. Bernice was the main link to my Chasidic childhood and no one else, not even the dear friends I'd made during and after the war, understood my roots as she did. I was thrilled to have her with me and we would be very close for more than sixty years in America and inseparable in our old age. Her husband, Mark, also a former Gerer Chasid, had received *smicha,* or rabbinical ordination, in Poland at age twenty. In America he would get a college degree and succeed in business, but his first job in Connecticut was no less physically demanding than was Martin's. Alongside Puerto Ricans, and blacks who had come up from the South, Mark worked in the tobacco fields, at that time a major crop in the Connecticut River Valley.

Through Jewish Family Services in Hartford, I arranged for a sofa and a bed for the Sobotkas and then put down a deposit on a larger apartment for my family in the same building, on the fifth floor. I got some basic furniture from the JFS for my place, too. But no one in our circle ever requested welfare or any other form of public assistance. We all had a fierce desire to make it on our own.

The rent on Charter Oak was $55 a month and to offset

some of that we took in a boarder. He was a single man whom I'd known in the Lodz ghetto, and whose wife and child and had not survived. He paid $20 monthly in exchange not only for his own room, but also for dinner with our family every night and for me washing his clothes. He was very thankful for the arrangement and always treated us with the utmost respect.

Our kindhearted Jewish landlord ran an appliance store and sold us a refrigerator and a small TV on credit. We missed Keney Park on Greenfield Street, but, finally settled in our own place, I felt that we were slowly moving up the economic ladder. Moses could now watch Howdy Doody and Mickey Mouse at home.

I brought in a little money myself at a part-time job in a bakery. On Sunday, his one day off, Martin could take care of our son. My brother-in-law, Joe, who worked as a barber, could help out on Mondays when his shop was closed. So I got hired for half the day on Sundays and Mondays, eight hours in all. Because I still wasn't fluent in English I couldn't deal with customers at the counter and had to work in the back of the store filling trays. But the job paid the nice wage of $8 a week. I put most of it toward household expenses, but also squirreled away a little bit out of every pay envelope into my own little *pushka*, or tin box—a rainy day fund.

It was vital to save every penny we could. I wouldn't even buy a piece of fruit if it wasn't on sale. In those days the super-markets were closed on Sundays, and they'd often mark down ripe produce on Saturday afternoon, thinking that by Monday it might go bad and have to be thrown away. So Saturday afternoon Bernice and I did our marketing. When Martin and I wanted to go to a movie, we'd share one ticket between us. That saved on childcare, too. He'd go in and see half the show while I'd take Moses by the hand and walk around the block a few times. Then he'd come out, give me the ticket as well as a quick plot summary, and take Moses. I'd enter the theater and later tell Martin how the story ended.

Any luxury had to be parceled out with the utmost care. How did we usher in the New Year of 1951? Martin and I had the whole gang over to our place for a party but we could afford only one éclair. So I sliced it thinly, added an orange wedge to each plate, and, voila, I had a classy dessert for eight. If I had one weakness it was shoes for Moses. I wanted him to have the best and bought them at Stride Rite for $10 a pair.

It was a hard life, but we were young, healthy, and strong, surrounded by good friends, *mishpoche* really, and filled with hope. Our English lessons continued on Charter Oak, now with another teacher, Mrs. Hartsmark, who was sent by a Jewish organization, and who thoughtfully brought along a couple of teenagers to care for our children while she tutored us. With every passing day we felt more comfortable in our adopted land. Martin, meanwhile, had proven himself an invaluable employee and was getting raise after raise. He still had to work incredibly long hours but in a couple of years was making almost $100 a week.

Then one night in the fall of 1951, he came home and told me that his employer, Kurt Leopold, was in deep trouble. He was accused of having sold freight cars full of rotten beef to the army during the war and now he had to face the consequences— criminal charges and civil suits. The Union Meat Company was heading toward bankruptcy.

Within a few weeks the plant closed and Martin was out of work. We were anxious as we pondered our options, but not in a panic. There were many immigrants around us, including our friends, who seemed to go from one job to another, usually improving themselves in the process. Mark Sobotka, for example, soon borrowed money to buy a grocery store and when that didn't work out, got a good position as a bookkeeper. Feliks Lubka had tried factory work and was now a pants presser; he would soon be a silk spotter. His brother Sam sold, cleaned, and mended hats, just as he had in prewar Lodz. Morris Zweibaum worked in a vodka distillery and put aside money toward the day he'd open a dry cleaning business.

But what was next for us? One possibility was to join our close friends Sam and Regina Spiegel who were now settled in Washington, D.C. Sam had a good head for business and urged Martin to join him in a retail venture, perhaps a liquor store. (Later, Sam would become a highly successful contractor for industrial heating, ventilation, and air conditioning systems, and outfit a number of major airports in the country.) We seriously considered moving to the nation's capital but in the end we couldn't bear to leave our friends in Hartford for a place we barely knew. In Washington, still somewhat of a provincial Southern city in those days, we would have the Spiegels, but knew few others, and there was nothing there like the close-knit survivor community in central Connecticut. In fact, Fred Jacobs, Mark Sobotka, and Sam Lubka would soon establish a formal organization of survivors in the Hartford area

More realistic, we thought, was a partnership with one of Martin's co-workers at the Union Meat Company, a nice fellow named Kenny, who also had been thrown out of work, and who suggested that he and Martin start a provisions business. Kenny, neither a Jew nor an immigrant, had been to our home for dinner a few times and I liked him a lot. Martin always spoke of him as a dependable worker and a good person. But ultimately we turned him down, too.

Another business proposition was put before us by Martin's older brother, Joe, and even though I strongly opposed it, my husband insisted that we accept. I thought that we were making a huge mistake; sadly, it turned out I was right.

Joe's plan was for us to go into partnership with him and his wife as chicken farmers in the stony hill country of southeastern Connecticut, about an hour's drive from Hartford. He had a piece of land picked out in the old rural town of Colchester. We hailed from the big, bustling city of Lodz and now we were going to live in a New England shtetl!

Some East European Jewish immigrants to America, especially earlier in the century, went "back to the land" for idealistic reasons. In Petaluma, California; Vineland, New Jersey; and other rural colonies, socialists and Zionists chose agriculture due to their love of the soil. Sometimes they even set up collective farms as an alternative to making *aliyah* and living on a kibbutz. That ideology was the furthest thing from our minds, however. For Martin and me, and Joe and Hana it was never intended to be anything but a way to earn a livelihood. Poultry ranching allowed us to acquire our own business overnight even though we lacked education and capital. But as we'd find out, to be farmers we'd have to sacrifice a great deal.

I went to Colchester only once before we took the plunge. The small town, founded in colonial times, was pleasant enough. It had tree-lined streets, a well-kept grassy commons, and a red-brick business block with a few stores. There was actually a good number of Jews in the area, in town and on the surrounding farms. There had been even more a generation earlier when "the Catskills of Connecticut" was half Jewish and every summer its rooming houses catered to tourists from New York and New Haven. So it was not as if we would be settling in Wyoming or South Dakota.

But when I saw the farm my heart sank. Our land, on the border of Colchester and another town to the north named Hebron, seemed out in the middle of nowhere, far from the main road and the nearest neighbor. We were getting only eighteen acres and even that included a pond and some swamps. There were just two small chicken coops, barely enough, it seemed to me, to support one family, let alone two.

The farmhouse was no gem either. A run-down, two-story structure, it needed a lot of repair and remodeling. The idea was for our family of three and Joe and his wife—as yet they had no kids—to live together in that dumpy dwelling. A second bathroom and kitchen would have to be built for them upstairs. But they'd have no separate entrance so I worried that my family would lose its privacy.

Lots of other alarm bells went off in my mind. It was a remote spot, a risky venture, and a future joined at the hip to my in-laws, neither of whom had impressed me with their decency in the past. We had gotten together with them often but they had never been part of my circle of Lodzers from Foehrenwald, the real source of my emotional well being. In fact, Martin and I would now be cut off from our best friends and able to see them only on weekends.

But Joe countered all of these objections by luring his kid brother with a rose-colored view of the riches that lay ahead. He foresaw not only adding a new, bigger chicken coop, but also fields of vegetables and plenty of livestock. "You'll make a fortune," he predicted.

I threw a fit and Martin and I had one of the biggest arguments of our marriage but I couldn't change his mind. Then I tried to get my way by begging but that, too, failed to budge him. If my security blanket was the Lubkas, Jacobs's, Sobotkas, and Zweibaums, his was one person, Joe, the much older, wealthier brother, whom he really didn't know very well, but whom he thought he could rely upon in times of crisis. It was a terrific tug of war that I lost.

I felt sick to my stomach while we signed the papers. Joe had his share of the down payment, $500, from his black market gains in post-war Germany. But we had to borrow that amount—from the kindhearted Kenny of all people, who was sorry to see us go. In the years ahead, as tough as it was, we made a point of paying him back, on time, every penny of that loan. Each family took a mortgage for $5,000 from the statewide Jewish Agricultural Society (which since 1900 had helped people like us get started), a debt that seemed crushing. Of course we knew that soon our liabilities would rise even higher as we borrowed for operating expenses and improvements to the house and farm, including a new chicken coop that we needed right away. And there was one more thing: the moving costs from Hartford to Colchester. For that I had to put up the little stash I'd saved painstakingly over the past two years; it had grown to $170 and it, too, had to be surrendered.

At times I tried to envision an upside to this turn in our lives. The fresh air and broad expanse of the country did appeal to me, especially in contrast to the plain fifth-floor walk-up in downtown Hartford. I thought of my youthful summers near Zdunska Wola and in fact the inviting landscape of eastern Connecticut wasn't that different.

Still, I didn't want to go. What I clung to was Martin and Joe's promise that we didn't have to live on the farm all that long. We'd make a pile and return to the city, they assured me. But it didn't work out that way. We remained chicken farmers for fifteen difficult years. And after all that time we left the same way we came, broke.

It was a life of drudgery. Because the farm never generated even close to the income we'd hoped for, Martin and Joe, and eventually I, too, were often forced to take other jobs to pay the bills. Joe worked as a barber in Colchester and Martin was hired by a local chicken slaughterhouse. When the Union Meat Company finally came out of bankruptcy, Kurt Leopold rehired my husband and he commuted from Colchester to the plant in Hartford. For a few years he held down that job as well as the one at the chicken slaughterhouse where he labored evenings and weekends. Later he would work in a plastics factory in the nearby country town of Moodus. This was the lot of most of the small farmers in Colchester; they could usually afford to work the land only part-time; they endured the tedium of the factory along with the rigors of the farm.

In our case, it meant that most of the responsibility of running the farm fell on my shoulders. At daybreak, before they went to work, our husbands fed the chickens from heavy pails of grain, but otherwise they pitched in only when they could. My sister-in-law, Hana, was allergic to the dirty, dusty air of the chicken coops, and never took to farm life, so her involvement was limited, too.

I was usually the one in the lead when something needed to get done. Given what I'd been through less than a decade earlier, I felt there wasn't anything I couldn't accomplish once I set my mind to it. The front steps of the farmhouse were sagging so I learned how to mix cement and rebuild them. The roof was leaking so I figured out how to install shingles and repair it. The linoleum in our living room was ugly and uncomfortable so I learned how to lay a carpet. Even before that, I learned how to drive and got my license and a ramshackle '42 Plymouth; I constantly had to pour water in the radiator to prevent it from overheating. I also sewed every chance I got. Martin bought me a used Singer machine for $5, Fred Jacobs provided me fabric from the shirt factory where he worked, and I made many of my family's clothes. I tried to be a real farm wife; we had only one cow but I made butter and cheese from the milk it produced.

Most demanding were the chickens, delivered to us as baby chicks from hatchery. It took about ten weeks for them to grow to full size and we typically raised more than 20,000 at a time. It was necessary to check on them regularly. I had to worry about the heat killing them in the summer, the cold getting to them in the winter, and disease all year around. There was also the danger of rodents, floods, and fires—a lot could go wrong. No minor chore was sweeping out the chicken shit. Usually dairy farmers, wanting to spread it on their fields as fertilizer, were happy to haul it off free of charge. But first we had to shovel it out of the coops into big heaps. The smell was sickening, worse than horse or cow manure. Still, as we used to joke, the odor would have been like French perfume if we were making money. Unfortunately, we weren't.

Theoretically, you could succeed in this business two ways: either through "broilers," sold for their meat, or through "layers" that you kept on the farm for their eggs. We started with broilers, and then switched to layers—requiring a lot more effort. Three times a day I'd have to go into the coops and gather the eggs. Sounds easy enough, but not when you consider the big, vicious roosters we had. Defending the eggs, they'd bite my arms, my legs, my rear end. Martin had to make thick cardboard shields for me to wear, otherwise I would have slowly been eaten alive. Of course, collecting the eggs was merely the first step. One by one, they still had to be cleaned, weighed, graded, and boxed. It was just our bad luck that as soon as we shifted to the more labor-intensive layers, new technology adopted by the big agricultural corporations drove the price of eggs down while the broilers became more valuable.

But worse than the financial setbacks was the loneliness. Especially during the long days, with Martin at work and my

Moses, Ellie, and Anne, on the right, on our chicken farm.

son away at elementary school, I could feel myself sinking into depression. Not least of all, I resented the separation during the week from our friends in Hartford. I was still in my twenties and thought another child might boost my spirits. Anne came along in September 1952, and Ileana, whom we always called Ellie, almost two and a half years later. The little girls gave us a lot of joy, but of course it was tough to raise three kids and manage the chickens at the same time. Two children were born to Hana and Joe on the farm as well. Eddie came into the world around the same time as Anne; and Rita was born about the time I had Ellie. Nine people—four adults and five children—lived in our farmhouse by 1955.

It was almost impossible to juggle everything. When I'd go to get the eggs during the day, I couldn't leave the girls home alone so I'd put them in the old Plymouth, drive the fifty yards or so to the coops, and lock them in the car while I did my work. It normally took a few minutes. But one time, rushing down from one level of the chicken coop to the other with two big baskets of eggs, my shoe got caught on a step and I fell down the flight of stairs. My body hurt terribly and as I lay there, I prayed I didn't have any broken bones and could get back to the car. Fortunately, I was just badly bruised and scraped; I could pick myself up and, dripping with egg yolk, tend to my children and return home. When Martin came home that night and heard the details of this close call, we both agreed that things had to change. He gave up his day job in Hartford in order to help run the farm although he continued to work part-time at the chicken slaughterhouse. Once the kids were all old enough to go to school, I, too, got a part-time job, behind the counter of a roadside luncheonette. I saved the money I earned in tips—nickels and dimes and every once in a while a quarter—to buy any clothes for my family that I couldn't make myself. As a high school student, Moses worked there as well, mopping floors and cleaning tables.

If the farm did not provide us with a livelihood, it was a nice benefit for our friends in Hartford. Almost every Sunday, when the weather was good, they'd drive out for a chicken Bar-B-Q and an outdoor card game. I also played Mah Jongh once a week with a group of women in Colchester, and was vice-president of the Hadassah chapter in our region, but the Sunday shindigs with the former Lodzers were the basis of my social life. We spoke of our wartime experiences, mostly in Yiddish and not in our mother tongue of Polish, a language evoking too many painful memories. These gatherings were a much-needed outlet because very few Americans, including American Jews, and including even our own relatives who had immigrated before the war, could relate to our suffering across the sea. Particularly in the early postwar years, those who heard our stories would quickly say something like, "That's too bad" and then change the subject. Only among fellow survivors could we hope to get any real empathy.

Yet during those get-togethers on the farm Martin and I could never fully relax. Sometimes we'd have to excuse ourselves to deal with the chickens. Once the gang met on the hottest day of the summer and just as we were all starting to unwind, Martin noticed some of the chicks dying from the heat. As the temperature rose, more and more of them dropped dead. Most though, ran to one end of the coop, where they piled up on top of one another, further increasing their body heat. Martin left our guests and spent the afternoon hosing down the roof of the coop in order to cool it off, but to no avail. We lost 5,000 birds that afternoon and the next day had to hire a guy to dig a deep pit to bury them.

During those years we drew a lot of emotional support from the Foehrenwald group, from Bernice and Mark, and from the Spiegels—Regina and her young daughter came up from Washington for a few weeks every summer. But our relationship with Joe and Hana, our housemates and closest relatives, was terrible.

Their marriage was a classic mismatch made by the war—Joe had been attracted to Hana by her beauty, yet they were as different as the sky and the earth—and they quarreled constantly. They first met in the Lodz ghetto but Hana had been deported there from Czechoslovakia, where she'd been raised in a wealthy, assimilated family; she didn't even speak Yiddish. In America she wanted nice furniture and jewelry, an occasional night on the town, and travel. Joe was just the opposite, a homebody who wouldn't part with a dollar. For a while, my sister-in-law tried to bring in a little extra money by selling magazines door-to-door, but then she gave up. The most downcast of any of us, Hana put on a lot of weight, let her good looks fade, and moped around.

But worst of all was the friction between them and us. Martin, between his job in Hartford and his moonlighting in Colchester, had a precious hour or two for dinner with the kids and me—and Hana insisted on mixing in. She was not a bad person but didn't know better than to sit downstairs in the tiny living room or even at our kitchen table and butt into our most intimate conversations. One time, when Martin told her to leave us alone and go upstairs to her floor, she flatly refused. My husband, who had quite a temper, grew furious and I feared he was going to slug Hana. He never did, but there were a lot of times when both of us seethed with anger toward her.

Joe, meanwhile, infuriated us with his stinginess. He tried to take advantage any way he could: the heating and electric bills, taxes and insurance, you name it. Nine years older than Martin, "the rich Libitzki" as he was known in Colchester (the brothers differed even on how they spelled their last name) thought he could intimidate "the poor Libitzky." But Martin sometimes stood up to the former ghetto cop and their shouting matches were loud and ugly.

I don't know how we lasted more than six years in the same house with Joe and Hana. There was barely a moment of harmony among us. Finally, after a big blow-up with Martin, they moved out and we divided the land. The two brothers, the only survivors of their prewar family of seven, didn't speak to one another for several years. The deep anger that flowed from their massive losses in Europe had divided and not united them. That hurt me so much that I ultimately brought them together although it remained a chilly peace.

Joe related to me far better than he did to Martin, so I thought I might be able to persuade him to be a little more generous to his family and the world around him. Several times I tried the old saw: "Joe, you can't take it with you." But he could, he always answered me: "I'm going to tie it to my belly and take it to the grave." Sometimes I wonder if he did just that. After his death in 1984, none of us, including his wife and kids could find the bulk of his assets. I was appalled when Joe's daughter, Rita, became a Jew for Jesus, but she rose a lot in my estimation by dutifully caring for her father during a long debilitating illness. Yet it was very hard getting anyone other than family members to attend his funeral; he was a man without friends.

A few years after our split with Joe and Hana, a disaster occurred that jeopardized even the meager income we made from farming. From the beginning, we had brought portable gas-fired heaters into the coops to keep the newborn chicks at the same temperature as if they were still cuddled by their natural mothers. The thousands of tiny birds were also warmed by a bed of sawdust. But one night in 1960 the highly flammable wood shavings got too near the burners and caught fire. Pixie, our family dog, barked loudly and we awoke to find two of the three chicken coops ablaze. The firefighters arrived in time to keep the flames from spreading to the house and they even saved the remaining coop; luckily it was the newest and largest of the three. But the other two were a total loss.

We'd planned to use the insurance money to rebuild the structures but the contractor we hired went bankrupt right after he'd dug the trenches for the foundation. It was yet another sign, as if we needed one, that this whole venture was cursed. Clearly, we had to find something new. The ruins of two chicken coops sent us that message every day.

Even so, it took us until 1965, the year Moses graduated from high school, to go into another line of work. While still living in the farmhouse, we opened the small Buttercup Bakery on Colchester's Main Street and specialized in donuts. Earlier,

Martin had cut way back on his other jobs and, in the employ of another bakery, learned how to make the donuts and run the business. I provided an important sideline, wedding cakes, which I decorated with elaborate icings including delicate roses. Anne, about twelve years old, helped, too; she turned out to be a born salesgirl.

The shop did well in the summertime when many people stopped for baked goods and coffee on their way out of town to the beach on Long Island Sound. But customers were scarce the rest of the year and after about eighteen months we made the hard choice of admitting failure and closing the store.

By now, despite all our hard work and initiative, our track record in the business world was pretty dismal. But fortunately we didn't give up. We found out about an opportunity thanks to our good friend Helen Kopman, a survivor whom we'd met in Hartford back in 1950 and whose story touched me deeply. In the Warsaw ghetto she had married at age sixteen less out of love than security; her husband, quite a bit older than Helen, was a baker, which meant she wouldn't starve. They were deported to Majdanek and later Auschwitz, and, thinking he'd died, she fell in love with another man as she recovered after the war in a TB sanitarium. But her husband eventually resurfaced and they resumed their marriage. They had had a baby in the Warsaw ghetto that had not survived; in America they raised a son and daughter.

We'd stayed in touch with the Kopmans over the years and in the 1960s they were running an immensely successful bakery in a strip mall in the Hartford suburb of Manchester. Helen told us of a run-down dry cleaners next door that could be bought cheaply and refurbished. Feliks Lubka, Morris Zweibaum, and Fred Jacobs had been operating dry cleaning establishments in and around Hartford for many years—Morris's was particularly profitable—so it hardly seemed like a strange idea.

We borrowed $11,000 to get started. Even though we were poor, we had good credit because my husband had always paid his bills, including those stemming from the ill-fated bakery venture. Feliks, as he had generously done with several other former Lodzers, taught Martin how to operate the machines, work with chemicals, and remove stains. Without our network of former survivors, most notably Feliks and Helen, we would not have been able to make this change in our lives.

For a year we still lived in Colchester and commuted to Manchester, about twenty-five miles away. Finally, in late 1966 a French-Canadian couple with about ten children took the farm off our hands. We bought a brand-new suburban home a short drive from our new business. It had a big kitchen with every modern convenience and spacious living and dining rooms; I'd now be able to host a proper Thanksgiving dinner or Passover Seder. The $30,000 price was far greater than what we'd wanted to pay, and the modest proceeds we got for the farm meant that we could make only a small down payment. But I'd found the palace of my dreams and couldn't pass it up.

For the first time my family had a real house like everyone else and didn't have to suffer the isolation and discomforts of rural life. Nor the humiliation. As farmers, we felt we were a cut below our city friends and now, in one stroke, we'd become equal. For all of the love in our circle of Lodzers, there was also a spirited competition among us and now Martin and I were no longer the shlimmazels of the group.

Moses was already away at college, but the girls made friends with kids on the same street and had plenty of activities nearby. In Colchester, although we'd celebrated Moses' Bar Mitzvah, we had not given our children much of a Jewish education—Martin had had a petty squabble with the leadership of the small shul and we stayed away for years—but in Manchester we quickly joined the Conservative Temple Beth Sholom. Ellie enrolled in its Hebrew School and became Bat Mitzvah two years later.

From the beginning our dry cleaning operation generated a lot of cash. The shop attracted customers from miles around and employed about half a dozen people. I played an important role, too, specializing in alterations. For once in our lives we began to see financial security on the horizon.

Indeed, we were doing so well that as early as 1968, Martin and I were able to undertake something that could only be a fantasy while we were raising chickens and pinching pennies in Colchester—a tour of Israel. It was such a high priority for us that we postponed buying some needed furniture for our new home in order to pay for the trip. In ten days we went all over the country, still in the glow of its miraculous victory in the Six Day War, and everywhere I cried with a feeling of homecoming. After all, my friends and I had nearly made *aliyah* after the war—this could very well have been our home. In Ashkelon, we had a wonderful visit with our sister-in-law Hana's brother and his family; they seemed a lot happier than Hana and Joe back in Colchester.

We also sent Ellie to Israel for a summer. Later we'd travel to Israel again and to Greece and Scandinavia, China and Malaysia, and Russia and the Black Sea. And we spent most summers in the Catskills.

When we left the farm I was in my early forties and my husband past fifty and my only regret was that we hadn't opened a retail business in the city as our friends had during the past decade and a half. But Martin had stubbornly thought that if we kept at it long enough, poultry ranching would eventually pay off and he'd show the crowd in Hartford that he wasn't a failure after all. I saw the bleak prospects of chicken farming early on, but bringing up three children, I was fearful of risking the little security it did provide us—a roof over our heads and food on the table—for an uncertain future somewhere else. The years slipped by, I went from being young to being middle aged, and we remained trapped by our circumstances. The freedom and fulfillment I'd expected in America eluded me. Aside from the war, which is obviously in a category of its own, the years in Colchester proved the worst of my entire life.

Looking back on that long period I often think about how it shaped my kids. It wasn't as bad for the girls as it was for Moses. They were fairly close in age and had each other. And despite all the feuding between Martin and Joe, our daughters remained very close to their two cousins. Anne and Eddie were born only nine days apart and Ellie and Rita were separated by only two months. Even after Joe's family moved out, our two households were linked by a path through the woods and along a brook that could be walked in fifteen minutes. The kids called themselves the Four Musketeers and played together all the time in a dilapidated shack that they fashioned into a clubhouse, and they had a tree house, too, cleverly designed by Eddie. Our girls even enjoyed the chore we gave them when they were old enough—cleaning and sorting eggs on a machine in the cellar. The rambunctious Anne would have even worked in the coops had we let her, but I was afraid she might fall prey to one of the many traps we set for rodents. Growing up on the farm, with its childhood pleasures, my daughters were blissfully ignorant of what they were missing elsewhere. When we finally left in 1966, Anne was fourteen and Ellie eleven.

Moses, however, was in Colchester until he went off to college and it pained me to see how lonely he was. A bit chubby, a bit awkward, and suffering from asthma, he needed more social stimulation than he could get on the farm. But the kids his age were four or five miles away and it was always hard for me to find the time to drive him to a friend's house and then pick him up. I did teach him games like badminton and Chinese checkers, but mostly he played cowboys and Indians in front of the house by himself; behind one tree he'd be the cowboy, behind another the Indian. Other than at school, and during the long ride on the bus every day, when the other kids sometimes picked on him, he didn't have much social interaction with other children.

We gave him tap dancing lessons, which hardly transformed him into the most popular kid in his class. Things did improve when we sent him to summer camp—we had to borrow for that— and when he was old enough to ride a bike. Yet nothing could take the place of the normal activities enjoyed by his "cousins" in Hartford. After school, they could just walk a short distance to a basketball court, say, and play a game with their friends. Sometimes they attended plays and concerts; in Colchester there was only one movie theater and we went to that infrequently. As

Moses carrying eggs on the farm.

he got older, Moses himself sensed a world of difference between city boys and country boys.

But he did very well in school and we encouraged him every step of the way. Perhaps it's a story typical of immigrant parents: with little spare cash, we nevertheless bought not one but two encyclopedias from a traveling salesman, *Compton's* and the *Britannica*. Moses read the former from beginning to end and pored over its atlas, which sat in a special slot in the bookcase that came with the set.

His greatest passion was for science, however, for which he won awards at every stage of his schooling. Around age ten he resolved to discover the cure for cancer. What choice did we have but to buy him a chemistry set, complete with microscope? He set up a little laboratory in the cellar and spent many hours experimenting—on mice. But before they could yield any medical clues, the mice had to contract the dread disease. This, my son thought he could accomplish by smearing their backs with nicotine, a grimy substance he collected from a cigarette-smoking machine he'd fabricated. Well, it didn't cause cancer in the little creatures, but they went wild, licking the nicotine off each other's backs. I paid little attention until a few of them escaped from their cages and soon got into the rest of the house. Because mice breed so rapidly, they caused us problems for years afterward.

Yet typically Moses was a highly responsible kid and we never thought twice about going out and leaving him at home to baby-sit the girls. We were also interested in what he was learning in class and, over our family dinner, we often discussed his schoolwork. Through him, we thus got a bit of an American education ourselves and also improved our English in the process. By the time he was in high school, during the civil rights movement and the beginning of the Vietnam War, we were having political discussions almost every night. We tried to be open to the progressive new ideas he was bringing home.

Because of the large difference in age between Moses and the girls—when he went off to college Ellie was still in elementary school and Anne had just begun middle school—we all treated him as a third adult in the family. After we moved to Manchester, my daughters experienced a lot of culture shock in making the adjustment from the farm to the suburbs—this was the late 60s, after all, and adolescent rebellion was commonplace—and Moses proved a big help in counseling them in a way that Martin and I could not. Being at Brandeis University at that time, it's not surprising that he was caught up in the counter-culture himself. He was such a nonconformist that it took all of my pleading to get him to forgo his plans to wear a bright green gown at his commencement. After his graduation in 1969, without a job awaiting him, and with only a few dollars in his pocket, he hitchhiked out to the Bay Area, seeking to make a life for himself there.

Only after we'd left Colchester could I appreciate that for all

Moses in the mid-1960s.

of the drawbacks of the farm, one positive thing it did was knit us closely together as a household. For the kids, there were far fewer distractions and temptations than in the suburbs, the city, or the college campus. It was a tough existence but we always made time for one another, a cohesive little unit of five. The focus of everything was our family.

Yet during the long, animated discussions we had, Martin and I shared with our children only bits and pieces of our wartime experiences. We weren't sure how they'd react to our painful stories or whether they could truly understand what we'd been through. Nor did they seem particularly curious about the family history, and the last thing we wanted to do was force it on them. Later I found out that they didn't want to cause us distress by dredging up such terrible recollections. In any case, they didn't ask and we didn't tell. Obviously, they were aware that we were immigrants, and that their grandparents had not survived, but they had no clue to the trauma their parents had endured.

Epilogue: **A Link in the Chain**

IT TOOK A LONG TIME before Martin and I were ready to tell our story to anyone outside our small circle of fellow survivors. Sometime in the early 1970s, when Moses was home on a visit from the West Coast, he accidentally came upon a short tape, a monologue I'd reluctantly made at the request of a school-teacher-friend who wanted to use it in one of her classes. My son turned on the tape recorder and heard me describe some of the details of the Lodz ghetto and Auschwitz. He was deeply shaken, but didn't ask me to elaborate. The time still wasn't right for a full exploration of what had happened during the war. All three of our kids were caught up in the here and now and that meant the youth culture. The American present was far more relevant than the Polish past.

In his early twenties my son, known as Richard since he was a baby, changed his name (back) to Moses, which he'd noticed on his citizenship papers when he wanted to travel to Mexico.

Even his driver license had said Richard. But the new name was neither an attempt to bond with his martyred grandfather, nor was it intended to bring him closer to Moses the lawgiver. Rather, it was a counter-cultural statement, an unusual name as an alternative to a typical one, something classical rather than something bland. And he felt more true to himself with his real name. In his early years in the Bay Area, he worked his way up the ladder in the emerging computer industry but he wore his hair long and lived in a commune. I flew out to Oakland and expressed my disapproval, but of course I could not change his life-style. In fact, he suggested that Martin and I join a commune! His Jewish heritage, certainly, was not a high priority at this time.

The girls, living with us in Manchester, had turbulent youths and it took them a while to settle down. They both married young in the mid-1970s, but neither marriage lasted more than a few years nor produced children. Martin and I were finally doing well financially, but the situation of our kids in a rapidly changing America weighed heavily on our minds. We, too, were more pre-occupied with the present than with the past.

Not until the 1980s, four decades after the terrible events had taken place, were my family and I ready to undertake our inquiry into a vanished world. Since then, we've taken great strides and I yet I know that we can never be at peace.

The first serious attempt to set down my personal history resulted both in pain and pride. In May 1982, in the company of an American-born Jewish friend, I drove from Manchester to New Haven where I was interviewed by the psychiatrist Dori Laub. A survivor from Romania who received his medical degree in Israel, Laub specialized in the trauma of Holocaust survivors. I appreciated his sensitive, gentle manner. He and his colleagues would conduct thousands of oral histories that later became the

Fortunoff Video Archive of Holocaust Testimonies at the Yale University Library.

I broke down in tears at several points during my hour-long narrative as I related the agonizing deaths of my parents and my own ordeal in the ghetto and camps. I told the doctor that I often lay awake at night trying to comprehend how I could have borne such pain and yet come out a sane person. But I also spoke of the loving childhood I'd experienced and the great respect accorded to my scholarly ancestors. I was proud to say whose daughter and granddaughter I am. The interview drained me emotionally but I also felt a sense of relief in having finally recorded my story.

In that initial account, I mentioned my own children more than a dozen times. I expressed my longing for them to know the history of their family in Poland—the glory and the horror. Yet my encounter with Laub, important though it was to me personally, was somehow not the proper vehicle to convey the story to Moses, Anne, and Ellie. As I told the doctor himself, "How can you fit six years of hell into sixty minutes?" Beyond that, I think my kids were fearful of viewing something so intimate and revealing. I told them of the tape but they showed little interest in it.

Still, the interview in New Haven did give me the confidence for a step I took in 1983: attending the American Gathering of Jewish Holocaust Survivors and Descendents in Washington, D.C. Two years earlier, a World Gathering had taken place in Jerusalem, the first assembly of its kind, and my friends the Kopmans participated and came home deeply moved by the experience. I can't recall why Martin and I didn't go; I suppose we felt we couldn't bear the flood of horrible memories. But I soon regretted my absence. I should have been there, I told myself, I should have stood shoulder to shoulder with my fellow survivors in the Jewish homeland. So when the American Gathering was scheduled for spring 1983, Martin and I, with Bernice and Mark Sobotka resolved to take part. And to my great joy, Moses and Anne, now in their thirties and both living in the Bay Area, offered to join us.

That event, held exactly forty years after the Warsaw Ghetto Uprising of April 1943, was pivotal in shaping my family's reaction to the Holocaust. Everything at the Gathering was endowed with significance and dignity. At a large indoor arena, the Capital Center in Landover, Maryland, President Reagan and Vice-President Bush, complete with Marine color guard, addressed the 20,000 participants. For us survivors, to be honored by America in that way meant an enormous amount. Elie Wiesel spoke as well and his sweeping hand gestures and riveting words made me think of what the Hebrew prophets must have been like. He was then chairman of the U.S. Holocaust Memorial Council, established

At the American Gathering. From right to left: Anne, myself, Sophie Lubka, Martin, Miriam Zweibaum, Bernice and Mark Sobotka, Helen Kopman and her daughter, Judith.

under President Carter, and was spearheading the construction of a great Holocaust museum adjacent to the Washington Mall. The groundbreaking was only a year and a half away.

At the American Gathering there was a registry of names, of course, and survivors also went around looking into one another's faces, hoping for a hint of recognition. Two former inmates of the Oederan slave labor camp remembered me but I could not recall them, nor could I make connections with anyone I'd known in Europe. But simply being a part of that reunion, and sharing it with most of my family, was vital. I felt supported in opening a box that had been locked for too long.

The trip to Washington was momentous in another way. As our family waited for the flight in Hartford's Bradley Airport, my cousin Bernice introduced Anne to a well-mannered young man whose family she had known both in Poland and America. Nathan Petrowsky, the dutiful son of a Connecticut dairy farmer and cattle dealer, was accompanying his parents, one of his two brothers, and sister-in-law to the American Gathering. His family's roots were in the rural village of Lask, coincidentally the birthplace of my grandmother Gerszt. Nathan and Anne were drawn to one another during the emotional trip, stayed in touch after they left Washington, carried on a coast-to-coast relationship for almost a year, and went to Israel together before getting married in the spring of 1984.

Ellie remarried around this time, too. Martin and I were initially upset that her second husband was not Jewish, but Paul Caruso's Orthodox conversion a year later, and the traditional Jewish wedding they had, went a long way toward healing the wound we felt. And Moses, now beginning to prosper in the Bay Area real estate business, married in 1984 as well. His bride was Susan Solomon, a fourth-generation Reform Jew from Dallas, Texas, who was the director of public relations for the Jewish

Federation in San Francisco.

My first grandchild, Sharon, was born to Anne and Nathan in March 1985, and Ellie gave birth to a girl later that year, Michelle. Three more grandkids would be born in 1988: Stacey Petrowsky, Paul Caruso, and Michael Libitzky. The start of a new generation gave me yet another reason to impart my story.

By the mid-80s, Moses had expressed his desire for a family trip to Poland. He had long been disillusioned with the left wing counter-culture in the Bay Area. Gradually his spiritual search led him to Judaism and his interest in modern history and politics brought him to Zionism. In June 1982, he visited Israel for the first time as the head of a young leadership mission from the Bay Area. It was on that intense journey, which departed on the day after the IDF's full-scale invasion of Lebanon, that he met Susan, whom he would marry two years later.

In the early 80s, Moses participated in a support group for children of Holocaust survivors, although he came away thinking that the impact of the Shoah on the second generation was exaggerated and often used by individuals as an excuse for personal or professional failure. He felt he was shaped more by his isolation on the chicken farm than by his parents' experience in the ghetto and camps. Still, he now wanted to travel to Eastern Europe to see the streets where Martin and I had grown up; he was also ready to visit the sites where his grandparents had been murdered.

I had misgivings about going with him. How could I again set foot in a country where Jewish blood cries out from the earth? And what could we see, anyway? Everything had been swept away by the war, I believed. On top of that, it would be a rigorous trip: we'd have to contend with a Communist dictatorship and crude living conditions.

But I was delighted with Moses' growing interest in the

family history, and I knew that he, and anyone else in the family who went, would get a lot more out of the trip if Martin and I came along. So I agreed, but we didn't leave for quite a while. We postponed the trip in 1986 and 1987 due to the Chernobyl nuclear disaster, and again in 1988 because of the arrival of three babies. Finally in June 1990, less than a year after the wall fell in Berlin and Solidarity came to power in Warsaw, we embarked on our expedition. It was Martin's and my first return to our native land in forty-five years. I had left there feeling utterly alone in the world and now I was coming back with my husband, two of my three children, Moses and Anne, and their spouses. Being with my family was the only way I could have endured the mental strain of that visit.

I was still fluent in Polish, as was Martin, but I had a ghostly feeling while speaking my mother tongue. From the moment we landed in Warsaw, I was overcome by anxiety, grief, and anger. And there was even more physical discomfort and ugliness than I'd expected. Poland had recently emerged from the shadows of totalitarianism, but it had hardly recovered from the damage done by more than forty years of a command economy and Soviet exploitation. We stayed in the best place Lodz had to offer, the Grand Hotel, but that name was a joke. The turn-of-the-century establishment, once the pride of the city, had badly deteriorated: the bathrooms were disgusting, the lighting was dim, and the walls held the cheapest artwork. When we walked out the door and onto Piotrkowska Street, which Martin and I remembered for its lively outdoor cafes and upscale boutiques, we were appalled by an empty, dead boulevard, its buildings covered with soot and grime. Even the famous palaces of Poznanski and the other textile magnates had fallen into decay. In the distance the hulking Stalinist-era apartment houses were further proof that our birthplace had lost its prewar luster. The first day I was so irritable that I was sorry I'd even made the trip. But as I surveyed the miserable conditions, there was some consolation: it seemed like a just punishment for Polish apathy and complicity during the Final Solution.

Perhaps that is an overly harsh judgment of an entire nation and, indeed, we met with a wonderful non-Jewish Lodzer, a former acquaintance of Martin's late brother. Joe had corresponded with him long after the war and now we were impressed with his decency and empathy. But when we went to our childhood homes and our dwellings in the ghetto, we encountered suspicion and even hostility from the populace. Sometimes children followed us on the street and shouted "*Jude, Jude,*" the German word for Jew heard during the Nazi occupation. At Zeromskiego 44, Martin knocked on the door of his old apartment and explained that he'd grown up there between the wars, and had now come from America to show the place to his family. The residents refused to let us in, plainly stating they were afraid we'd come to take back the furniture! But worst of all was the anti-Semitic graffiti we saw all over town, even in the former ghetto, even on the walls of the building where my father had starved to death and where my mother and I had suffered so much. Swastikas, skinhead emblems, and anti-Jewish slogans told us that the old hatred was still there.

Not surprisingly, the vast Jewish cemetery on the outskirts of the ghetto was in deplorable condition. Lodz's tiny Jewish population, old and impoverished, could hardly care for almost two hundred thousand graves. True, some restoration work was underway, due to the philanthropic efforts of Sigmund Nissenbaum, a survivor of the Warsaw ghetto who had made a fortune in Switzerland after the war. Toward the end of our trip we met him by chance in the only remaining synagogue in the Polish capital and expressed our gratitude to him. But Nissenbaum could barely begin the enormous task of restoring the hundred-acre Lodz cemetery, to say nothing of a thousand other neglected and vandalized Jewish graveyards across Poland.

So we saw the dead victimized again. Many of the tombstones were overturned and in pieces. Thick, fast-growing vegetation had covered up many others. Litter was strewn about and quite a few of the memorials were desecrated with Nazi symbols. Tens of thousands of Jews, like my father, had been buried in that cemetery during the ghetto period with no markers at all except for flimsy tin plates that were long gone. During the war, some families had surrounded a loved one's grave with old metal bed-frames and we saw some rusted ones still in place.

Thankfully, the graves of my grandfather, Abraham Katz, and his only son, Yankel, who had both died in the ghetto, were

In the cemetery on the edge of the Lodz ghetto, Moses and Anne comfort Martin and me at the double grave of my grandfather Abraham Katz and his son, Yankel.

marked by a dignified double tombstone. It was erected by Bernice and Mark in 1945 even before they were married. We found that place and recited a tearful Kaddish. Then we moved on to the spot where my father had been buried in 1943, where as a teenager I had promised myself I would return some day. I was now sixty-six, but I had made it back. It wasn't hard to find the plot, whose location I still remembered—just within the brick wall of the cemetery and on a direct line with the massive arched entryway. The grave was all that Martin had of his father-in-law, and Moses and Anne had of their *Zayde*.

Again, we said Kaddish and I nearly collapsed from heartache, but my kids steadied me in the warm sun. Later that day, we went to the *Gemine*, the Jewish community council (which my grandfather had served as a member of the governing board) and arranged for a *matsevah*, a gravestone, for my father, Shlomo Gerszt. Moses and Susan and Martin and I resolved to return a year later for its unveiling, the customary practice for traditional Jews, and, indeed, we made that trip as well.

We were all pained that Martin had no knowledge of where his parents had been buried in 1942 and thus could not commemorate them as I could my father. During our trip, he kept his anger inside him and rarely showed self-pity, or much emotion at all, as he related the atrocities he'd witnessed. When we walked past the former hospital in the ghetto, he told us he had personally seen the SS raid that took place there in September 1942. Patients still in their medical gowns, including small children, were thrown out of upper-story windows he said calmly. But my husband's tough exterior was finally pierced when he reflected on his favorite sister, Ita, deported from the ghetto to the Chelmno death camp in June 1944. He broke down when he told Moses and Anne of his last conversation with her. Thinking that no place could be worse than the ghetto, he had advised her not to go into hiding, but to get on the train. He now revealed to us all that he'd been racked by guilt ever since he learned of her fate in 1945.

My family could not leave Poland without visiting Auschwitz-Birkenau, about an hour's drive from Cracow. But the morning we were to set out, Moses and Anne came to our hotel room and suggested that Martin and I stay behind. Standing again in the place of mass execution might be too much for us, they said. I was touched by their concern, but we decided that having come so far already, we should show our kids everything, even the darkest spot on earth.

The brick buildings of the camp known as Auschwitz I were unfamiliar to Martin and me; in August 1944, the cattle cars had taken us directly to Birkenau, about two miles away. Auschwitz I was now a museum filled with tourists and my family walked through rooms of glass display cases, which held piles of hair, shoes, eyeglasses, and suitcases, all confiscated from newly arrived inmates at the railhead. These were powerful reminders, but I was disappointed that so little attention was given to the Jewish dimension of the catastrophe. Jews accounted for the overwhelming majority of the 1.5 million people gassed here, but you wouldn't know it from the memorial plaques put up in the Communist era dedicated simply "to the victims of Hitlerism." Photos of the victims hung throughout the museum, but I couldn't find one with a Jewish name or face. Some of the buildings were devoted to the suffering of particular groups and there was one for the Jews but it was small, and the last one in a long row.

We drove on to Birkenau, which in 1990 many visitors missed, and for hours we were virtually alone in that desolate place. That was the actual site of the extermination and many of the hundreds of barracks remained. My block, number 25, was gone, but I showed my family a similar one still standing; it, too had no bunks and no floor, and I explained how my "Auschwitz sisters" and I lay directly on the muddy ground. "The *Blockaelteste*, holding a cane, strutted up and down a platform just like this one," I told them. But I still wasn't sure if people who had not experienced this, even the children of survivors, could truly grasp it.

We walked to the far end of the camp, to the remains of the crematoria, blown up by the SS in the last days before the liberation. The concrete rubble was the only *matsevah* we had for my mother, and a million other Jews, incinerated at that spot. I saw my kids and their spouses weeping openly with me and now I knew why I'd made this trip.

After I returned home from Poland, I vowed to myself that I'd make my story known to a wider audience. And an incident soon occurred that made it even more pressing to bear witness. It had its roots in Cracow where we toured the sixteenth-century synagogue of the Talmudic sage Rabbi Moshe Isserles, known as the REMU. There we met a couple from New Jersey who had just visited Auschwitz and were eager to talk about it with survivors. The husband soon mentioned he was a journalist for the *Asbury Park Press* and asked if he could interview Martin and me for an article. We told him of our wartime experiences, Susan added a bit about our trip, and the well-written piece appeared after we got back to the States. Soon after it was published, I received a long letter addressed to "the Libitzkys of Manchester." We'd been quoted in the paper about our fear of returning to a country in which so much Jewish blood had been spilled, and although we also stressed that we'd always rejected revenge, a Polish-American was furious that we had cast her native land in a bad light. She wrote that Poland suffered under Nazi oppression because of its "innocent, good-hearted" decision to shelter millions of Jews over the centuries. "Shame on you!" she went on, "No one really wanted you people, but Poland was ... hospitable."

Even worse was to come. The New Jersey journalist wrote a second article describing the deluge of neo-Nazi hate mail he'd received since his original report appeared. Holocaust deniers condemned him for having believed the words of a "monumental liar hustling hatred."

I responded by making Shoah education and remembrance a major part of my life. Having moved permanently to South Florida in 1991, I became one of many survivors in that region to speak to teenagers about the Holocaust. I'd declined such invitations in Connecticut, but now I accepted. I've gone to top private schools, like Pine Crest in Fort Lauderdale, but also racially mixed public high schools, some in rough neighborhoods. Everywhere, I've been met with respect and gratitude from principals, teachers, and students alike. Their letters of appreciation fill an entire drawer. Of course the Holocaust is a part of the school curriculum—Florida is a national leader in that regard—but the educators have indicated to me that nothing can replace the testimony of an eyewitness. Especially rewarding in recent years have been the Awareness Days conducted by the Jewish Federation's Holocaust Documentation and Education Center. Attracting hundreds of high school students, the event features a keynote speaker, films, and then roundtable discussions over a light lunch, with survivors interspersed among groups of ten to twelve kids.

In 1998, Martin and I felt ready to undertake another trip to Poland, this time with the March of the Living. This exceptional program, permanently endowed by Leo Martin, a survivor from Lodz living in Florida, brings high school students to Poland during the week of Yom Ha-Shoah on their way to Israel where they commemorate Memorial Day for the fallen soldiers, and cel-

ebrate Independence Day. Seven thousand young people participated the year that we went—Israel's fiftieth anniversary—and
I was proud that almost 30% of them came from South Florida.
My husband, past eighty, and I were guides on separate buses,
and I heard from the kids that his warmth and kindness deeply
affected them. It was the first time either of us had seen Treblinka
and I felt that even the stones were weeping. At Majdanek I was
haunted by the crematoria and barracks, most them still intact,
and almost in plain sight of the major city of Lublin.

Our day at Auschwitz-Birkenau, despite the profound sadness, was also one of triumph. I was awestruck as I saw thousands
of youths in blue and white jackets, proudly holding aloft Israeli
flags. I marched with them from Auschwitz into Birkenau, along
the same train tracks that each day in the summer of 1944 had
transported thousands of Jews by cattle car. I was one of those
utterly powerless victims. This time, Israeli planes protectively

Martin and I at Auschwitz on the March of the Living, April 1998.

With Martin, before his illness, and our three children: Ellie, on the left, Moses, and Anne.

flew overhead. Prime Minister Netanyahu, wrapped in a *tallit*, recited the *Sh'ma* and addressed the marchers as did Israeli President Ezer Weizman. Throughout the day, loudspeakers intoned the names of the quarter-million children killed there. At the crematoria I lit candles for my mother as I had done with my family in 1990. I inscribed the name Chana Gerszt on a small wooden panel that each of us was given to mark the death of a loved one, and left it among hundreds of similar "matsevot" at the site of the ovens. I also planted a little Israeli flag. Then I resumed the sacred work of educating the teenagers in my charge; I did my best to get across to them what it was like to be an inmate of Block 25.

The March of the Living was the last time I would visit Poland or Israel. In the new century I became consumed by a problem like none I had ever faced before. Martin gradually began to show signs of dementia and was diagnosed with Alzheimer's. For

With my family at my fiftieth wedding anniversary in 1996. From left to right, back row: Nathan, Anne, myself, Martin, Ellie, Paul, Susan, and Moses; front row: my grandchildren Sharon, Stacey, Paul, Michelle, and Michael.

several years, with the help of medical attendants, he and I were able to live together in our oceanfront condo, but in 2007, after his condition noticeably worsened, my family and I made the decision to place him in a nearby nursing home. It was one of the hardest things I've ever had to do. Although I visit him almost every day, I will never adjust to living apart from the man I married in 1946. He still recognizes me although he has no memory of the last time I was there. But it is for my sake as much as his that I need to see him regularly. He is also visited often by the rest of our family, including our great-granddaughter, Madison, born to Ellie and Paul's daughter Michelle in 2007.

Martin's buddies, Sam and Feliks Lubka and Morris Zweibaum are gone now, as are Miriam Zweibaum and Regina Lubka. But her sister-in-law, Sophie Lubka, lives on and she and Sam and Regina Spiegel (who still volunteers at the U.S. Holocaust Memorial Museum in Washington) are my closest friends. For more than a decade in Florida I also had a "sister." She was really my older cousin, the widowed Bernice Sobotka, who lived four floors below me in our Pompano Beach high rise. We often reminisced about the old days, including the incomparable cookies our Hasidic grandmother, Ruchel Katz, baked for Shabbes seventy-five years ago, although no matter how hard we tried, we couldn't replicate them. Sadly, Bernice passed away on May 1, 2010, less than two weeks before Regina Lubka died. My children comforted me during that month of mourning but I have not yet come to terms with the loss of these two pillars of my life.

Because of the responsibility I feel toward Martin, now in his mid-ninties, I have ruled out overseas travel. On occasion, I still speak about the Shoah to high school students, but I don't feel that I can join the March of the Living anymore or accompany my family members on further tours of Poland.

But it's done my heart good to see that my kids have continued the journey of discovery on their own. In mid-2007, Moses, a top lay leader in the East Bay Jewish community and active nationally in AIPAC, was invited with Susan to spend a week in Poland as part of a delegation of VIPs headed by the philanthropist Tad

With Bernice

Taube. My son and daughter-in-law's experience, coinciding with the gala Jewish Culture Festival in Cracow, was very different than the one they'd had with Anne, Nathan, Martin and me seventeen years earlier. This time they met with scholars, rabbis, activists, and artists who reflected a new Poland—democratic and oriented toward the west, pro-Israel and sensitive to Jewish concerns. Poland, they explained, as a member of NATO and the European Union, is now safer and more prosperous than at any time in its history; it has taken a new turn.

I was highly skeptical about all of this and will never be able to trust the country that was not only rabidly anti-Semitic before the war, but that also permitted murderous attacks against Jews after the liberation. I might befriend an individual Pole, and I dispensed some charity to strangers when I was in Lodz in 1990, but the Polish nation, like Germany, cannot redeem itself in my eyes. I need only recall the Polish peasants interviewed in Claude Lanzmann's classic film *Shoah* of 1985, who expressed to a returning survivor their approval of the Final Solution.

In the summer of 2009, Moses traveled yet again to Poland, his fourth time there, and brought Ellie, who had missed the family trip in 1990. They went as participants in a study tour of Warsaw, Cracow, and Budapest conducted by Lehrhaus Judaica, the San Francisco Jewish Community Center, and the Taube Foundation. On a special pre-tour excursion, they and several others visited Lodz and its environs for three and a half days.

I was amazed at how much they saw and how much they learned in a country I'd regarded as little more than a wasteland. I found out that dedicated historians, archivists, genealogists, tour guides, and museum curators—most of them young Poles—have recovered a great deal of the Jewish past. In a recently restored cemetery in my grandparents' town of Zdunska Wola, my kids were led to a tombstone inscribed with our family name. In the

*Moses and Ellie examine a nineteenth-century gravestone with
the Gerszt name in the Jewish cemetery of Zdunska Wola*

Polish State Archives in Lodz, they found the registration cards of most of my family, and our next-door neighbors, the Mests, with whom I was so intertwined. On Brzezinska Street they found the attic in which the five of us hid before being transported to Auschwitz.

Moses and Ellie also visited my childhood home, over our family business in Gorny Rynek, where my parents moved in as newlyweds more than a century ago. It is once again a pleasant area, and most, although not all, of the anti-Semitic graffiti visible in 1990 is gone, as it is from our dwelling in the ghetto. Lodz has changed a lot, they reported. They stayed in the Grand Hotel, which was only marginally better than in 1990, but the very week of their visit, a plush ultra-modern hotel opened in the sprawling Manufaktura shopping center, a tasteful rehab of the Poznanski textile plant. It draws customers from all over the Continent. The city's elegant palaces are being restored, too, and Piotrkowska Street is once again a Mecca for commerce and culture.

But if Lodz has revived, and Jewish visitors and their

descendents can feel more comfortable and welcome than we did in 1990, Jewish life can hardly return. Only murals remain to mark the sites of the great synagogues of my day, only statues exist as a reminder of the great Jewish contribution to industry and the arts before the war. The inescapable fact is that the Lodz Jewish community now numbers only a few hundred souls. When I was growing up, it was literally a thousand times as large as it is today.

It is not only because I am part of the shrinking remnant of former Jewish Lodzers that I feel a responsibility to tell my story, but also as the sole survivor of my father's huge extended family. Like all of my ancestors and descendents, I am only one link in a long human chain. But I am the one that fate chose to make the leap from Poland to America, and from tradition to modernity.

I appreciate better than most how the world has changed. Every time I use email, drive on the Florida highways, or turn on the air conditioner, I'm reminded of the stark differences with the era of my youth. And that's the least of it. The greatest contrasts with prewar Poland are that I live as a proud Jew, in a democratic country, with the State of Israel thriving as well.

In other respects the world has not changed. Genocide has occurred since the war, even in Europe, and is taking place in Africa now. Anti-Semitism continues to rage and Israel remains embattled. Sometimes, I think of my life as a warning bell for the twenty-first century. It shows the devastation that radical evil can leave in its wake and how vulnerable we all are to savagery.

I hope it also illustrates something about strength as well as suffering. For my kids, their children, and their children's children, I want my past to be more of a gift than a burden. When I returned to Auschwitz for the first time Moses was by my side and he said to me: "You and Dad have given us the confidence that *whatever* happens, we'll make it through."

Afterword and Acknowledgments

I FIRST MET EVA LIBITZKY at the Piedmont, California home of her son, Moses, who had suggested that I co-author her memoir. He had earlier told me the rough outline of her almost six-year-long ordeal—the Lodz ghetto, Auschwitz-Birkenau, the Oederan slave labor camp, and Theresienstadt—and I expected to be able to read the suffering on her face. Instead, I found a vivacious octogenarian, full of energy and laughter, and enjoying life's pleasures. For the next four years, as we worked together on this project, I continued to be in awe of her ability to leave bitterness and anger aside, even as she delved into an unspeakably horrific past.

I interviewed her during two subsequent visits she made to her children and grandchildren in the Bay Area, and also six times in her home in Pompano Beach, Florida. We compiled about eighty hours of audio-tape, which I transcribed myself in order to become familiar with her thought and speech patterns. I then used the transcript as the basis of the foregoing narrative, which Eva edited numerous times.

But this book also owes a great deal to archival sources; never before in my extensive work with Holocaust survivors have I obtained such a wealth of documentary material.

In Lodz, Poland, Moses and I were able to access a directory of almost all the 175,000 Jews in that city's infamous ghetto, including their addresses before and during ghettoization, their dates of birth, and dates of death or deportation. In the Lodz State Archives we found the identity cards of Eva and nearly all of her friends and family indicating their birthplace, occupation, and marital status.

Such evidence helped me piece together the story and also stirred Eva's memory. Yet nothing prepared me, or the Libitzky family, for the stunning revelations yielded by the International Tracing Service, the 150-million-page archive in Bad Arolsen, Germany, recently digitized and opened to researchers at the United States Holocaust Memorial Museum. In August 2009, I spent two weeks in Washington, D.C. as part of an international team of twelve scholars assembled by the USHMM's Center for Advanced Holocaust Studies to assess the value of the vast and unwieldy ITS archive. In the course of my work, I traced the trajectory of one individual through the Shoah—Eva Libitzky

Employing two different software programs specifically designed to access this colossal repository, I found the results of medical tests performed on Eva in Auschwitz; her transport list from Birkenau to the Oederan slave labor camp; her identity card as a prisoner there; her release forms from Theresienstadt; and her records in the Foehrenwald DP camp. The basic elements of the story she told more than six decades later were thus resoundingly confirmed for me by scans of original documents that I viewed on a computer screen in a museum near the Capitol Mall. Several of them are included in the appendix to this volume.

The archive also corroborated a fact I'd gleaned from Eva's records in the Lodz State Archives: she and Wolf (Vevik) Mest were married by the chairman of the Lodz Judenrat, Chaim Rumkowski, in April 1944, four months before they were deported to Auschwitz. Her spouse of the past sixty-four years, Martin Libitzky, is actually her second husband.

Eva had never spoken of Vevik to Martin or to her three children, now all middle-aged and with children of their own. But in her many interviews with me, she had gradually revealed how, despite her religious mother's strong objections, her love for Vevik had flowered in the ghetto. Eva was prepared in this book to break her silence about that relationship and share its secrets with her family and the general public. However, the wedding itself (a perfunctory ceremony with many other couples on the same evening) had actually receded from her mind. But now, two thirds of a century later, she was improbably faced not only with archival evidence of the marriage, but also with a raft of other documents identifying her in the various camps as Eva Mest rather than her maiden name, Eva Gerszt.

It was an eerie, unsettling moment for her. But within a few days, the same archive that had shaken Eva so deeply also provided a measure of psychological closure. In post-liberation Prague in June 1945 she had been told of Vevik's death, but now, from Washington, D.C., came an official record of the date, place, and cause of his murder.

At an emotional family gathering at her Florida home, all three of Eva's children expressed to her their happiness in having learned that amidst the torment of the last months of the Lodz ghetto, their mother had found a loving partner. In finally grasping the fullness of Eva Libitzky's Holocaust journey, they, too, achieved a measure of closure.

I was aided by an abundance of sources in addition to the

original records I discovered at the USHMM. The Lodz ghetto is particularly well documented because in 1940 Rumkowski established a Department of Archives to gather information, mostly on daily life, for an eventual history. An outstanding group of historians, ethnographers, journalists, and photographers participated in the project, which resulted in an almost day-by-day account, a collective diary of despair lasting until the eve of the ghetto's liquidation in mid-1944. Later edited by the eminent historian of Polish Jewry Lucjan Dobroszycki, *The Chronicle of the Lodz Ghetto, 1941-1944* (Yale University Press, 1984) proved an indispensable resource for me. I would like to thank YUP for permission to reprint from that volume the map of wartime Lodz that appears in these pages.

Also of enormous help was the companion volume, *Lodz Ghetto: Inside a Community under Siege* (Penguin Books, 1989) edited by Alan Adelson and Robert Lapides. Drawing upon not only the Rumkowski Archives and German administrative records, but also ghetto dwellers' private journals, this anthology supplements the mountain of facts in the *Chronicle* with compelling personal testimony.

The brief excerpts in *Lodz Ghetto* led me to the contributors' full-length works as I sought to place in context the suffering experienced by Eva and her family. *The Diary of David Sierakowiak* (Oxford University Press, 1996), nearly burned for heat, preserves the acute observations of a teenager who died of malnutrition in mid-1943. Josef Zelkowicz, a middle-aged literary critic and folklorist who was murdered in Auschwitz in 1944, also kept a diary, *In Those Terrible Days* (Yad Vashem, 2002), filled with vignettes about the cruelty of the Jewish bureaucracy as well as the German soldiers. The vital perspective of a Viennese intellectual deported to the Lodz ghetto is provided by Oscar Rosenfeld's notebooks, *In the Beginning was the Ghetto* (Northwestern University Press,

2002); he, too, was killed in Auschwitz.

Memoirs of survivors written many decades after their confinement in the Lodz ghetto were also highly useful. The Berkeley writer Lucille Eichengreen, transported in October 1941 to Lodz from her native Hamburg, has penned two revealing autobiographical works: *From Ashes to Life* (Mercury House, 1994) and (with Rebecca Camhi Fromer) *Rumkowski and the Orphans of Lodz* (Mercury House, 2000). In the latter, she recounts being sexually abused by the Eldest of the Jews. Arnold Mostowicz was a practicing physician in the ghetto and he describes the appalling medical conditions in *With a Yellow Star and a Red Cross* (Vallentine Mitchell, 2005). In *My Survivor* (Friends of March of the Living, 2003), the philanthropist Leo Martin, who permanently endowed the March of the Living, provides rich detail about the factory work he performed as a youth in the ghetto.

The most valuable survivor memoir for my purposes was the sensitive *Stolen Years* (Lerner Publications, 1981) by Sara Zyskind, a bright girl from a prosperous Orthodox (although not Chasidic) family in Lodz, who like Eva was ghettoized in her hometown, deported to Auschwitz, and later transported to a slave labor camp in Germany. She immigrated to Palestine after the war and at the age of twenty served in the Israeli Army during the War of Independence. Another survivor, the Canadian-based Chava Rosenfarb, has illuminated wartime Lodz through poetry and fiction. Especially evocative is her novel *Tree of Life* (University of Wisconsin Press, 2004-06), a trilogy originally written in Yiddish in 1972.

A scaffold for Eva's story was also provided by three full-length social histories of the ghetto. Robert Moses Shapiro deserves much credit for translating and editing the monograph of the distinguished Holocaust scholar Isaiah Trunk, *Lodz Ghetto* (Indiana University Press, 2006), first published in Yiddish in

1962. I am grateful to IUP and the USHMM for allowing me to reprint here the street map in that book of the city of Lodz. A fascinating recent study is *Ghettostadt: Lodz and the Making of a Nazi City*, by Gordon J. Horwitz (Harvard University Press, 2008), which contrasts conditions in the ghetto with the rest of Litzmannstadt, intended to be a model city of the Third Reich. I was further assisted by the well-illustrated *Lodz Ghetto, 1940-1944* (Vadecum, 2006) by the Polish historian Julian Baranowski.

An article raising the issue of gender is "The Status and Plight of Women in the Lodz Ghetto," by Michal Ungar in *Women in the Holocaust* by Dalia Ofer and Lenore J. Weitzman (Yale University Press, 1999). Two telling photo albums are Mendel Grossman's black-and-white *With a Camera in the Ghetto* (Ghetto Fighters' House, 1972) and Henryk Ross's *Lodz Ghetto Album* (Boot, 2004) in color. Grossman survived the ghetto but not the war. His huge photo archive was saved and sent to Israel but sadly most of it was lost during the Egyptian invasion in 1948. Several of the extant photos are included in this volume courtesy of the USHMM.

While the ghetto was the most formative period of Eva's life, I also researched her Chasidic youth in Lodz before the war. Two publications on Poland's large, vibrant Gerer sect, and its confrontation with modernity were especially useful: Gershon Bacon's "The Politics of Tradition: Agudat Yisrael in Poland 1916-1939," in *Studies of the Center for Research on the History of Polish Jews* (Magnes Press, 1996); and the Ph.D. dissertation of Robert Moses Shapiro, *Jewish Self-government in Poland: Lodz, 1914-1939* (Columbia University, 1987).

An excellent collection of articles on the changing socioeconomic condition of Lodz Jewry over four generation is *Jews in Lodz, 1821-1939*, edited by Antony Polonsky (1991, 2004), in the authoritative series *Polin: Studies in Polish Jewry* (Littman Library of Jewish Civilization). I.J. Singer's epic novel *The Brothers Ashkenazi* portrays a Jewish family of wealthy, ambitious industrialists rising in tandem with Lodz itself in the late nineteenth and early twentieth centuries. On the Jews in interwar Poland, I learned much from Celia Heller's classic *On the Edge of Destruction* (Columbia University Press, 1977).

Eva's experience in Auschwitz-Birkenau was illuminated for me by the landmark study *Values and Violence in Auschwitz* (University of California Press, 1979) by the Polish sociologist Anna Pawelcznska who focused on the coping mechanisms of women. A concise distillation of the vast literature on the iconic death camp is *Auschwitz: A New History* (BBC Books, 2005) by Laurence Rees.

Far more difficult to investigate was the small and little-known slave labor camp of Oederan, Germany, where Eva was an inmate for more than half a year, but I gleaned much from a new publication of the USHMM, the monumental *Encyclopedia of Camps and Ghettos: 1933-1945* (2009). At that institution, I was also able to screen videotapes, made by the USC Shoah Foundation Institute, of several survivors of Oederan. A further glimpse into the camp was provided by Professor Steve Klepetar's haunting poem "Cat-Woman of Oederan," inspired by his mother's experience there.

For an understanding of the immediate post-liberation period in Poland I turned to Jan T. Gross's definitive *Fear: Anti-Semitism in Poland after Auschwitz* (Random House, 2006). In exploring Eva's years in the DP camp, I consulted *Life between Memory and Hope* (Cambridge University Press, 2002) by Zeev Mankowitz.

On the lives of Holocaust survivors in America, my main source was Walter B. Helmreich's inspiring *Against All Odds* (Simon and Schuster, 1992). Regarding the Libitzkys' improbable decade and a half as chicken farmers in Connecticut, I learned the history of their rural community through an article by Alexander and Lilian Feinsilver, "Colchester's Yankee Jews," in *Commentary* (July 1955).

In the course of writing this book, I traveled to many of the key locations in Eva's Holocaust journey: Lodz, Auschwitz-Birkenau, Theresienstadt, and Prague. My visit to Lodz and its environs was especially rewarding because of the guidance of a young, dedicated Polish academic, Maciek Kronenberg, who expertly led me through memorials, cemeteries, synagogues, and archives. Thanks to him, I came away not only with a deeper understanding of the tortured history of Lodz, but also with some hope for its future.

I consulted with three scholars of the Lodz ghetto as I composed the manuscript: Irena Kohn of the University of Toronto, Robert Moses Shapiro of Brooklyn College, and Michal Ungar of Bar Ilan University. I met and studied with all three at a conference held at New York's YIVO Institute for Jewish Research in the summer of 2006 and I thank that institution for inviting me to such a worthwhile forum both for learning and networking.

This volume also owes much to personal interviews. Many years before this project began, Eva and Martin were each interviewed twice, and those videotapes were essential as I conceptualized their life histories. In May 1982, the fifty-eight-year old Eva was filmed in conversation with Dr. Dori Laub, affiliated with the Yale Medical School, and the following year Martin was queried by one of Laub's associates, Dana L. Kline. In November 1996, Eva was interviewed by Nancy Solomon, and Martin by Helene Mandel-Schull, both of the Southeast Florida Holocaust Memorial Center (now the Holocaust Documentation and Education Center) in Hollywood, Florida. Martin's two videotapes contain some inconsistencies, but taken together they hold more biographical information about him than does any other source. I was also aided by the long, unedited home movie of the Libitzky-Petrowsky trip to Poland in 1990, and I thank the family for sharing it with me. It was far less tedious to watch than they thought it would be.

My own audiotaped conversations with Eva, during a two-year period beginning in March 2006, constitute the core of this book. They were enriched by the keen memory, intelligence, and wit of her first cousin Bernice Sobotka (earlier Bronka Katz), who sat in on nearly every hour of the many long interviews in South Florida. A few years older than Eva, Bernice was more privy to some the family's prewar accomplishments and tribulations. It was my privilege and good fortune to have interviewed both of these strong women together. I deeply regret that Bernice did not live to see the publication of this volume.

I also conducted interviews in the New York and New Jersey homes of two other close companions of Eva in Europe: her dear friend Sophie Lubka, and Martin's cousin Henry Rotman. Also helpful in answering the many questions I posed to them during the past few years were Regina and Sam Spiegel, Fred Jacobs, and Steven Zweibaum. Eva and I thank all of these informants for their input and their interest in our project.

The three Libitzky children, Moses, Anne, and Ellie, not only provided invaluable information and insight about their parents, but also carefully read the manuscript in draft and made many beneficial suggestions. Eva's daughter-in-law, Susan Libitzky, and son-in-law Nathan Petrowsky, were similarly engaged in helping me craft the narrative.

Several others improved the book with their advice and raised our spirits with their encouragement: Dorothy Shipps, Bobbi Leigh Zito, Harold Lindenthal, Donna Rosenthal, Robert Moses Shapiro, and Megan Trank. I am especially grateful to June Brott of Oakland, California, an author, editor, and teacher of writing, who meticulously copy-edited the manuscript.

Above all, Eva and I thank Moses for the responsibility he has taken to keep alive his family's story and add to the historical record of modern Polish Jewry. This book could not have been written without his support.

Fred Rosenbaum
Brooklyn, New York
Berkeley, California

Appendix

A Note on the History of Lodz and its Jews

An industrial colossus and Poland's second largest city by the middle of the nineteenth century, Lodz was an inconsequential rural village only a generation earlier. As late as 1821, four hundred years after its founding, the population stood at merely 767. But the town grew much faster than even such dynamic European manufacturing hubs as Manchester, Glasgow, Lyon, and Hamburg. By 1865, Lodz would reach 32,500 and soar to 630,000 by the eve of World War I when it accounted for more than 30% of the industrial output of the entire Polish Kingdom.

One sector of the economy drove this extraordinary growth in population and productivity—textiles. By 1900, more than half of all Polish workers employed in this industry lived and worked in Lodz. The huge fortress-like brick factories and the adjacent neo-Renaissance mansions of their owners were the most visible buildings in town. The smoke from the chimneys and the clatter of the machines permeated entire neighborhoods. And class conflict between the mill workers and the company proprietors swayed the city's politics. Virtually everything in Lodz revolved around the manufacture of cloth.

Many factors accounted for the dominance of this one industry. It began with a government policy in the 1820s to invite skilled weavers from nearby Prussia into Poland, so that fine fabric could be domestically produced and not have to be imported at exorbitant prices. Lodz, surrounded by much open space, with building materials such as brick and timber in abundance, and ample supplies of river water nearby, became a prime location for the construction of factories. Later, highways, rail lines, and an electric tramway (the first in Poland) made the city even more attractive to entrepreneurs.

In the 1830s, the ethnic German weavers and their families, arriving en masse in horse-drawn carts, constituted the large majority of Lodzers. But the following decades saw an influx of Poles and Jews, also attracted by the rapidly expanding economy. The appeal of the burgeoning city was such that it soon became known as the "Promised Land," later the title of a famous novel by Wladyslaw Reymont and film by Andrzej Wajda about the industrial revolution in Lodz.

Sometime in the second half of the nineteenth century, the Poles overtook the Germans as the largest group but they did not become the majority. The census of 1897 shows the Jews (a good number of them immigrants from Lithuania) were around 30%, the Germans 20%, and ethnic Russians 2.5%. However, the Russian impact upon Lodz was greater than that small percentage indicates, because the Kingdom of Poland was ruled by the Czar from 1815 until World War I. Polish sovereignty disappeared during that century and Lodzers came under the authority of the many Russian officials in town. Beyond that, the vast Czarist Empire was the main market for Lodz's textiles, so Russian buyers and agents also flocked to the city. Four different languages were commonly heard in the streets, stores, and offices.

Compared to the rest of Eastern Europe in the late nineteenth century, Jews fared well in multi-ethnic, multi-lingual Lodz. Of course, anti-Semitism was deeply ingrained in the minds of the Poles, Germans, and Russians. But no single religion held sway; together the Jews, Protestants, and Russian Orthodox outnumbered the Catholics in Poland's second city.

Early on, there had been restrictions on where Jews could live in Lodz. (They were confined to the Old Town and the sandy, run-down Baluty district, coincidentally the location of the ghetto created by the Germans in 1940.) But in 1862, a year after serfdom ended in the Czarist Empire, the Jews of Lodz gained the right to live anywhere, purchase property, and even hold office. At that time, too, the special taxes levied on Jews were abolished.

Political freedom opened the gates to commercial opportunity. Jews became highly conspicuous in the economic "take-off" which Lodz experienced during its golden age from 1865 to 1914. In that half century the population grew seventeen-fold, as did the number of people employed in the textile factories, and many of the leading manufacturers were Jews. Although the very biggest, Karol Scheibler, was of German extraction, a close second was Israel Kalman Poznanski, who employed about 7,000 workers in Lodz by the turn of the century. The Poznanskis were pioneers in replacing handlooms with steam-powered machines, and their enormous profits were reflected in the family's stately palaces and ornate mausoleum, landmarks in Lodz to this day. Other Jewish textile titans included the Rosenblatts, Ginsbergs, Konstadts, Jarocinskis, and many others. In the early years of the twentieth century, twenty textile companies in Lodz employed more than a thousand workers; half of these firms were owned by Jews, the other half by Germans.

Of course, the boom in textiles boosted many other industries: real estate, banking and finance, shipping, utilities, and much else. Jews were highly active in those fields, as well as in small business, and before World War I accounted for 55% of the city's merchants. These included Eva's parents and maternal grandparents who operated a flourishing grocery store in southeastern Lodz.

When Shlomo Gerszt and Chana Katz married around 1908, they must have felt fairly hopeful about the future even in a non-Jewish neighborhood, even under the rule of the Czar. Of course, as Chasidim they were conscious of how distinct they were from the gentiles, but nevertheless they saw the Jewish community as a permanent thread of the city's rich tapestry.

World War I, however, ushered in three-quarters of a century of turmoil and trauma for Polish Jewry. Lodz changed drastically under the German occupation from 1914 to 1918, which destroyed much of the industry, ended the lucrative trade with the Czarist Empire, and caused the Russian inhabitants to flee the enemy troops. After the war, many of the ethnic Germans abandoned Lodz as well; their percentage of the population dropped by half to 10%. The Jews still accounted for three out of every ten Lodzers, but six of the other seven were now Polish Catholics.

At the Paris Peace Conference in 1919, Poland was finally awarded its independence after more than a century under foreign domination. But the Polish nationalists who came to power proved to be harsh rulers themselves. The government and the Church clearly considered the non-Polish minorities (mostly Jews, Germans, Ukrainians, Belorussians, and Lithuanians) as undesirable second-class citizens, and acted accordingly with punitive legislation and inflammatory innuendo. In Lodz, business activity gradually picked up in the 1920s, but Poles often resented that, even in a sovereign Poland, almost all of the leading businesses were in the hands of Germans and Jews. Although, as Eva remembers, there could still be cordial relations among individuals of different backgrounds, on the group level coexistence gave way to hostility. In the turbulent 1930s, the worldwide Depression, the death of the benevolent dictator Marshal Pilsudski, and the threats from neighboring Nazi Germany and Soviet Russia further aggravated the internal dissension and anti-Semitism in Poland. Jews were verbally attacked by public officials and physically assaulted by roving hoodlums. Like Eva, the overwhelming majority of Jews who lived through interwar

Poland felt unwanted and unsafe in their homeland.

To be sure, by the early decades of the twentieth century, Jews had made a deep impact on Polish culture, just as they penetrated Polish industry. Lodz, for example, spawned such prodigies as the pianist Artur Rubenstein, the illustrator Artur Szyk, the painter Jankel Adler, and the poet Julian Tuwim. But especially in the interwar period, the Poles were as averse to Jewish artists and intellectuals as they were to Jewish bankers and industrialists. Whether they wrote in Yiddish or Polish, whether they painted portraits of traditional rabbis or scenes of the bucolic Polish countryside, the Jewish creators of culture were invariably considered alien.

The factious interwar years were of course followed by a nightmarish half-century of German occupation and Soviet domination. Then, with the collapse of communism in 1989, the Poles again became master in their own house. But the minority groups, sources of such irritation in the First Republic, have been virtually absent in the Second. Because of Nazi genocide, forced migration, and redrawn borders, postwar Poland has been one of the most homogeneous countries in Europe with around 97% ethnic Poles.

The ethos of Poland since the fall of the Berlin Wall is very different than that of the country that was dismembered in 1939. It has not only forged strong economic and political ties with the West and Israel, but it has also celebrated its diverse past. As the journalist Kostek Gebert puts it, while the East Germans could look over the wall for a model, the Poles rather looked back across history, and found a paradigm for the twenty-first century in the pre-World War I mix of coexisting nationalities.

Nowhere in today's Poland is more homage paid to the pluralism of the past than it is in Lodz. Every year since 2002, the city has proudly hosted a Festival of Dialogue of Four Cultures, an elaborate ten-day program of music, drama, film, art, and poetry, all intended to showcase Lodz as the product of Russian, German, Jewish, and Polish influences. As of this writing, Lodz is a strong competitor to be designated by the EU as the European Capital of Culture for 2016, the epitome on the entire Continent of fruitful exchange among cultures.

Although foreign businessmen again descend on the city, along with western tourists and shoppers, the multi-ethnic Lodz of 1900, with its large, creative Jewish population, cannot be replicated. But it can be commemorated.

Fred Rosenbaum

Samples of the Documentary Record

Through the Lodz State Archives and the International Tracing Service, recently opened to researchers at the United States Holocaust Memorial Museum, it was possible to document Eva's Holocaust odyssey. Although she was born in 1924, the year of birth in some of these records is given as 1922 or 1923.

1. Registration card in the Lodz Ghetto (1944)

Eva's marriage to Wolf Mest on April 23, 1944 is indicated after the word "Anmerkungen" or notes. (From the Lodz State Archives)

2. An inmate of Block 25 in Birkenau (September 1944)

This list indicated medical tests such as blood, urine, sputum, and stool samples. Eva, number 60, has no memory of these tests having been performed. (From the International Tracing Service of the USHMM)

3. The transport list from Auschwitz to Oederan (October 1944)

Eva is number 54628. The late Regina Lubka, whom she met on that transport and who would become her lifelong friend, is listed above her at number 54620 under her maiden name Regina Jakobowitz. (from the ITS of the USHMM #10796318)

No.	Surname	First name	Place / DOB	Notes
3	Szymkiewitz	Anna	Litzmanstadt 29.5.25	9.10.44 Oederan
4	Titenschneider	Pola	Radomsko 5.3.12	9.10.44 Oederan
5	Kutner	Guta	Sierota 1.3.22	9.10.44 Oederan
6	Gotthelf	Hella	Litzmanstadt 15.5.24	9.10.44 Oederan
7	Federmann	Paulina	Litzmanstadt 4.3.15	9.10.44 Oederan
8	Zwirn	Edith	Litzmanstadt 16.1.25	9.10.44 Oederan
9	Zuckermann	Rosa	Litzmanstadt 18.11.20	9.10.44 Oederan
54620	Jakobowitz	Regina	Litzmanstadt 17.12.21	9.10.44 Oederan
1	Schächter	Bella	Lublin 24.10.24	9.10.44 Oederan
2	Rosenberg	Rosa	Litzmanstadt 5.12.25	9.10.44 Oederan
3	Rosenberg	Eva	Litzmanstadt 12.5.18	9.10.44 Oederan
4	Kaczka	Gitla	Patrikau 5.4.17	9.10.44 Oederan
5	Kaczka	Dora	Patrikau 22.2.18	9.10.44 Oederan
6	Schumirei	Era	Litzmanstadt 14.8.18	9.10.44 Oederan
7	Naumark	Ester	Kolo 3.10.18	9.10.44 Oederan
8	Mast	Eva	Litzmanstadt 28.2.22	9.10.44 Oederan
9	Malinska	Ester	Litzmanstadt 5.4.44	9.10.44 Oederan
54630	Faskowicz	Genia	Litzmanstadt 15.12.14	9.10.44 Oederan
1	Krieger	Marilla	Litzmanstadt 26.1.26	9.10.44 Oederan
2	Passlaska	Gitla	Lututow 8.5.21	9.10.44 Oederan
3	Landowitz	Ruchla	Litzmanstadt 10.4.24	9.10.44 Oederan
4	Wolken	Berti	Wien 16.1.25	9.10.44 Oederan
5	Goldwasser	Rose	Lewise 12.4.20	6.1.45 Hertine 10.10.44 Hertine

4. The Prisoner's Personal Card in the Oederan Slave Labor Camp (October 1944)

The abbreviation "FLOSS." stands for Flossenberg, of which Oederan, near Dresden, was a sub-camp. (From the ITS of the USHMM #11077843)

5. Record of Internment in Theresienstadt (May 1945)
(From the ITS of the USHMM #5064609)

ÚSTŘEDNÍ KARTOTÉKA — TRANSPORTY.

*Osoby, které prošly Terezínem před koncem války · podle publikace MSP,
repatr. odbor: „Terezín - Ghetto — díl I."*

Mest Eva

rozná data: 28. 2. 1923

bydliště před deportaci *Łódź*

folio v knize „Terezín" 326

V.

356

6. Death Record of Wolf (Vevik) Mest (May 1945)

On a list identified as "the dead of unknown nationality of concentration camp Gross-Rosen, sub-camp Riese," Eva's first husband is number 217. His date of death is May 22, 1945, two weeks after the end of the war in Europe. The cause of death is "dystrophy" atrophy of the muscles due to malnutrition. (From the ITS of the USHMM #141021)

			- 4 -	*82*		
174	19097	Kotek Peszach	unbek.	27. 1.45	unbk.	Dörnhau
175	,62453	Jutkovics Asriel	"	"	"	"
176	20601	Feikind Leib	"	"	"	"
177	29050	Rosenzweig Riven	"	"	"	"
178	33869	Glück Eugen	?	"	"	?
179	45566	Simches Simon	"	"	"	"
180	33363	Steinberg Samuel	?	"	"	"
181	33113	Grünhut Aladar	"	"	"	"
182	34027	Kalmanovics Alex.	"	"	"	"
183	25880	Herzberg Mosek	"	"	"	"
184	19022	Koppel Moritz	"	"	"	"
185	20644	Grünwald Heinrich	."	"	"	"
186	23693	Jungbeer Mendel	"	28. 1.45	"	"
187	23610	Salamon Max	"	"	"	"
188	20898	Fogel Chajim	"	"	"	"
189	39301	Felsmann Lazar	"	"	"	"
190	41338	Stern Isidor	"	"	"	"
191	34449	Wengraf Bernard	27. 5.04	29.1.45	Herzschw.	Fürstenb.
192		Adlerstein Jakob	19. 6.23	2. 6.45	Flek	Wüsterg.
193		Barna János	7. 4.19	23. 5.45	TBC	
194		Beni Laszló	7. 2.98	20. 5.45	Flec.	"
195		Chitter Géza	14.11.28	20. 5.45	"	"
196		Deutsch Israel	22.12.25	2. 6.45	Ditrophie	"
197		Dominigini Hans	25. 1.29	20. 5.45	Fleck.	
198		Fixler Eisig	21.11.96	31. 5.45	Ditrophie	"
199		" Benö	13. 9.03	25. 5.45	"	"
200		Förster Slama	26.11.06	6. 6.45	Sepsis	"
201		Friedmann Chajim	22. 4.22	25. 5.45	Distrophie	"
202		Gad Salamon	27. 5.25	27. 5.45	"	"
203		Coldblatt Gustáv	2. 5.24	10. 6.45	"	"
204		Graumann Osias	21. 8.03	4. 6.55	"	"
205		Halberstadt Lendört	7.11.16	30. 5.45	Pneumonie	"
206		Halpern David	17. 7.97	14. 6.45	"	"
207		Junger Josef	19. 6.25	23. 5.45	Dystrophie	"
208		Kandel Ladislaus	14. 9.23	21. 5.45	Flecf.	"
209		Katz Marton	22.11.96	28. 5.45	Dystrophie	"
210		Karlo Marte	25. 1.11	unbek	"	"
211		Kringel Karl	5. 3.03	27. 5.45	"	"
212		Lippmann Leib	11.11.18	12. 6.45	TBC	"
213		Löwinger Laszló	19. 9.99	24. 5.45	Distrophie	"
214		Mai Moses	24. 4.03	24. 5.45	Pneumonie	"
215		Merton Abraham	23. 1.98	26. 5.45	Dystrophie	"
216		Merin Smul	15.12.18	26. 5.45	Herzchw.	"
217		Mest Wolf	7. 5.16	22. 5.45	Dystrophie	"
218		Mühlbauer Zoltán	13. 1.96	9. 6.45	Flecf.	"
219		Oprandovics Chajim	10. 1.21	27. 5.45	Dystrophie	"
220		Pinkas Fischel	8.12.00	23. 5.45	Flecf.	"
221		Rado Andor	25. 3.24	19. 5.45	Dystrophie	"
222		Rosen Israel	7.12.10	18. 5.45	unbekannt	"
223		Selzer Majlach	23.12.02	5. 6.45	Dystrophie	"
224		Stern Josef	13. 7.25	23. 5.45	Flecf.	"
225		Schönwald Josef	18.12.18	1. 5.45	"	"
226		Schwartz Mano	25. 2.89	27. 5.45	Sepsis	"
227		Tabasnik Ernö	3. 5.99	22. 5.45	Flecf.	"
228		Tobias Erich	14. 4.98	27. 5.45	Dystrophie	"
229		Wedel Karl	9. 6.05	24. 5.45	Flecf	"
230		Weinberg Samuel	15.11.26	23. 5.45	TBC	"